alternative vegan

Healthy Plant–Based Recipes That Break the Rules

marie reginato

founder of 8th and Lake

PAGE STREET
PUBLISHING CO.

PAGE STREET
PUBLISHING CO.

First published in 2017 by

Page Street Publishing Co.

27 Congress Street, Suite 105

Salem, MA 01970

www.pagestreetpublishing.com

Distributed by Macmillan, sales in Canada by The Canadian Manda Group.

21 20 19 18 17   1 2 3 4 5

ISBN-13: 978-1-62414-467-7

ISBN-10: 1-62414-467-5

Library of Congress Control Number: 2017937023

Cover and book design by Page Street Publishing Co.

Photography by Marie Reginato

Printed and bound in China

As a member of 1% for the Planet, Page Street Publishing protects our planet by donating to nonprofits like The Trustees, which focuses on local land conservation. Learn more at onepercentfortheplanet.org.

This book is dedicated to my readers.

You have shown me the greatest support, love and constant enthusiasm for the blog and recipes I create. This book is all for you. I hope that it inspires you to keep living a life filled with crazy delicious and vibrant foods, keeping it real and keeping it fun. Thank you for taking me on this wild ride, making my dream come true.

contents

Introduction

If you were to go back in time and explain to a high school friend of mine that in ten years I would write a cookbook, one that celebrates plant-based foods nonetheless, they'd laugh in your face and walk off to meet me at the vending machine for a second pack of chocolate peanut butter cups.

Because in those days, I was slinging back peanut butter cups as if the industry's fate rested in my ability to consume as many as I possibly could in one week's time. You see, I was not the poster child for healthy eating. To really put it into perspective, this was 2005 and wellness and healthy eating were on the cusp of a universal explosion.

Everything shifted when I left San Francisco to study in Italy, a country where pizza, pasta and gelato reign—my kind of paradise. After landing in Florence with major sticker shock from the horrible exchange rate, I realized I could not afford these luxuries for every meal. Out of necessity, I started to cook—slowly, very slowly. During the following year, I made friends with an Italian family. I taught them English, and they taught me Italian in return. Once a week, their daughter would pick me up on her classic Vespa and we'd venture to her family's home for a quintessential Italian feast. One evening over a three-hour meal of stuffed eggplants, stewed winter squash and handrolled zucchini bites; they entrusted me with two markers that define Italian cooking:

1) Buy only enough fruit and vegetables to last you a few days.

2) Eat only the foods that you truly love – the ones that taste utterly delicious.

I was 21 years old and coming from a Costco-size purchasing strategy; these concepts were revelations to me. Over the year, I was taught the essentials of plant-based cooking—how to make fresh tomato sauce with sprigs of earthy basil and roasted seasonal vegetables as well as stews rich with spices and herbs. Without realizing it, I hadn't gone near a pack of peanut butter cups in months, and best of all, the recipes I was embracing were abundant in whole-food ingredients. The foods were simple to the bone but exploding with flavor. I took all the cooking notes and memories I could consume, came back to the States, started a food blog and quite literally, everything changed.

Pre-Italy my life was a revolving ritual of doughnuts for breakfast, frozen pizza for dinner and plenty of fast-food enjoyment. When I returned to the States, I dabbled in and out of a vegan lifestyle. Then I played around with a vegetarian one. But after some time and plenty of experimentation, what I found to be truly satisfying and sustainable was a diet rich in whole foods with room for a little seafood and eggs—never depriving myself of either. As I adopted a looser approach to food by removing diet labels and food banishment, an appreciation for food and cooking blossomed. Instead of punishing myself for the times when I'd slip up or didn't follow a strict diet, I came to understand that food is truly about enjoyment and knowing what is a healthy alternative for *your* body. Nowadays, my food philosophy centers around mostly fruits and vegetables, although if a craving for pizza comes on, I'm going to make sure it's the best damn slice of pizza I can find and I will absolutely enjoy it.

That is the intention of this cookbook—one of plant-based inclusion. A "one size fits all" approach to food and diet simply does not work. We all have different needs, desires and taste buds. Celebrating the fact that you can still eat healthy while enjoying your favorites is what this cookbook is all about. This is a cookbook for those who want to continue eating healthy but with an approach to food that is modern and inclusive, while being able to enjoy a plant-based lifestyle with room to also savor your favorites every so often.

Marie Reginato

7

My Food Philosophy

I adore food. One of the greatest pleasures in life is to experience, explore and enjoy food with a curious appetite. In Italy, I explored ways of cooking that centered on plant-based goodness, and I fell hard for this approach. When I headed back to California, this is the style I happily continued—creating delicious meals that are comforting and familiar, yet grounded in health. Recipes that focus on nourishing your body through an abundance of natural foods. The colors, the vibrancy and the beauty that each unique vegetable and fruit offers is glorious.

While most of the time I gravitate towards a veggie-rich meal, I also adore seafood and eggs from time to time. That is why over three quartes of the recipes in this book are vegan with a section on seafood and eggs. Hence, *Alternative Vegan*—vegan-inspired recipes for most days, with the option of incorporating a few favorites. This is a sentiment I strive for. Food is a very personal endeavor, so instead of labeling or trying to fit perfectly within the confines of one diet, I implore you to eat with an open mind while celebrating the foods that excite you.

For the times when you'd like to throw an egg or a beautiful piece of fish on a dish, go right ahead! It's all about making food enjoyable and finding what suits you.

Letting go of the all-or-nothing mentality toward food is truly liberating, especially if you're eating a mostly vegan diet. Instead of beating yourself up for having a day when you're not completely plant-based, try to not be so hard on yourself. Find room for flexibility in your diet. And when that moment comes when you'd like an egg or a piece of meat, don't feel bad about it. Fully embrace and savor the meal. Life is too short to be so strict with your diet to the point where it deprives you of all satisfaction.

That is why all the recipes here are healthy, delicious and most importantly, forgiving. So if you want a poached egg to accompany your Zesty Sweet Potato Hash (page 162), then why not go for it! At the end of the day food is about you, your needs, your taste buds and what excites *you*. That is how healthful eating becomes sustainable.

It's about enjoyment more than anything else. I promise you that with some guidance on flavorful food and spice pairings, coupled with simple ways in which to cook veggies you will fall hard, just as I did in Italy. These recipes will help get you there. All in all, this cookbook celebrates a realistic and delicious approach to food that happens to be great for you.

A Few Notes on the Recipes

To make it a bit easier, at the beginning of each recipe there is a symbol indicating whether the meal is vegan, vegetarian and/or gluten-free.

V vegan recipe

VEG vegetarian recipe

GF gluten-free recipe

Many of the recipes in the book are easily adapted from vegetarian to vegan or vice versa. If you prefer a completely vegan option, feel free to swap the ingredients below for their vegan counterparts:

1. Farm Egg to Flax Egg or Chia Egg (page 188)

2. Ghee to Coconut Oil or Olive Oil

3. Greek Yogurt to Coconut Yogurt

4. Chocolate to Vegan Chocolate

5. Honey to Maple Syrup

I also suggest reading the entire recipe beforehand, gauging the steps, the cooking tips and ingredients that are necessary to make the meal. Nothing is worse than getting halfway through a recipe and then discovering that you have to soak nuts for 7 hours! We've all been there.

Happy cooking!

Three Hero Meals

These are the recipes that I turn to most often when I'm pressed for time or when my creativity in the kitchen is zapped for the day. The recipes below are intended as blueprints, guiding you through how to make each recipe based on the ingredients you already have on hand.

This section is broken down into one example recipe for each meal of the day: breakfast, snack, lunch or dinner. These are dependable and doable recipes that I hope inspire your cooking endeavors, arming you with a few tried and true meals for your weekly repertoire.

Anatomy of Smoothies

When making a smoothie it's easier on the blender to first add in your liquid, then your greens, flavor boosters and finally the frozen fruit. This way there is enough liquid to start blending.

1. Choose your liquid: 1 cup (240 ml) of any nut milk, coconut milk or coconut water

2. Choose your greens: 1 big handful of spinach, kale or romaine lettuce (I prefer spinach as it blends well with no added flavor)

3. Add in any extra flavors or health boosters: 1 tablespoon of nut butter, yogurt, chia seeds, flax seeds, plant-based protein powder, fresh herbs (basil or mint leaves), cacao powder, cinnamon, etc.

4. Choose your fruit: 1 frozen banana + 1 cup any berry or fruit

5. Blend and enjoy immediately!

*View full recipes on pages 22, 125, 126, 129

** For a no-fuss plant-based milk recipe, try Hemp Seed Milk: simply add 1 cup (160 g) raw-shelled hemp seeds and 3½ cups (840 ml) water in your blender and blend for 1 minute. Store in an airtight jar in the fridge. It will stay fresh for about 3 to 4 days.

Anatomy of Energy Balls

My go-to snack! These little guys take all of five minutes to make and the flavor combinations are endless. They're delicious and packed with whole food goodness—great for that 3:00 p.m. energy slump.

1. Choose your dried fruit (used as the base and binder): 1 cup of dates, apricots, raisins or figs, etc.

2. Pick your nut or seed: 1 cup of any nut or seed (cashew, almond, hazelnut, walnut, sesame, etc.)

3. Choose your flavoring: 1 teaspoon of cacao powder, vanilla powder, cinnamon, zest of lime/lemon, etc.

4. Blend and roll into little balls, and store in your freezer.

*View full recipes on page 121

Anatomy of Buddha Bowls

This is what I like to call modern fast-food. Take any leftovers you have and add them into one big ol' bowl for a hearty afternoon meal.

1. Choose your greens: 1 cup of arugula, spinach, kale, romaine, etc.

2. Pick a creamy topping: 1 scoop of hummus or guacamole

3. Add in roasted vegetables: ½ cup of sweet potatoes, cauliflower, eggplant, carrots, beets, Brussels sprouts, etc.

4. Choose a protein: ¼ cup of beans, hard-boiled egg, piece of salmon/tuna, etc.

5. Add in a whole grain: ½ cup of brown rice, quinoa, wild rice, farro, etc.

6. Top with dressing: any dressing from pages 112–115

*View full recipes in Chapter 5 (page 99)

1

Breakfast, It's What's for Dinner...

Lunch, snack time or really anytime.

A wise person once proclaimed (on Instagram) that "sleep is essentially a time machine to breakfast"… and they say you can't find great advice online.

Breakfast is all encompassing—it does and has it all. Can you think of another occasion where you have your choice of fluffy pancakes, juicy baked apples with ginger cream, citrusy bircher muesli and a Bloody Mary, all before 10:00 a.m.? I don't think so. For this reason alone I am thoroughly perplexed by those rare beings who don't embrace a hearty breakfast. I mean, do you really want to pass on that stack of hot Spiced Waffles Topped with Stewed Apples and Hazelnut Crunch (page 14) first thing in the morning? Maybe it's just the seeming inconvenience of it all, in which case, I have a whole chapter dedicated to those mornings, too. Whichever it may be, here is my collection of breakfast recipes, from Honey-Poached Pears (page 25) to Apricot and Lavender Scones (page 17). Each will leave you in anticipation of your morning alarm and for breakfast to finally commence.

Spiced Waffles Topped with Stewed Apples and Hazelnut Crunch

These waffles were actually never intended for this book. In fact, I never even thought about including a waffle recipe. What a shame that would be – a breakfast section without waffles? That's like eating a birthday cake without any frosting or going to an 'NSYNC concert where, surprise, Justin Timberlake isn't even performing and you're stuck listening to the other four guys (what were their names again?). Luckily, the original porridge recipe didn't make the cut, allowing us to enjoy the stewed cinnamon apples atop a stack of warm waffles! Speckled with coconut sugar and made with spelt flour, these crispy, golden waffles are utterly delicious with just a touch of sweetness. These fully loaded waffles are what I crave during the weekdays and whip up first thing Saturday morning. Oh, and don't forget to finish it off with a healthy dose of melted ghee and crushed hazelnuts for a ridiculously decadent breakfast. This is what they call a crowd pleaser.

MAKES 4 WAFFLES / V

For the waffle batter

1 cup (240 ml) almond milk

2 tbsp (30 ml) coconut oil, melted

1 flax egg (page 188)

Pinch of sea salt

1 cup (120 g) spelt flour

½ tbsp (6 g) baking powder

3 tbsp (36 g) coconut sugar

For the stewed apples

2 tbsp (30 ml) ghee, or coconut oil if vegan, plus 2 tbsp (30 ml) for topping

2 apples, thinly sliced into matchstick pieces

4 tsp (16 g) coconut sugar

1 tsp cinnamon powder

1 tsp vanilla powder or extract

Handful of hazelnuts, roughly chopped

Pinch of sea salt

Start by making the waffle batter. In a medium-sized bowl, whisk together the almond milk, melted coconut oil, flax egg and pinch of sea salt, until combined. Now add the rest of the batter ingredients to the bowl and mix well. Set the batter aside while you prepare the topping.

In a medium-sized sauté pan on high heat, melt the ghee (or coconut oil). Bring the heat back down to medium and stir in the apple slices, coconut sugar, cinnamon, vanilla, hazelnuts and a pinch of sea salt. Sauté for about 5 minutes, or until the apples have softened but are still a bit firm.

Cook the waffles in your waffle iron. When they're ready to be served, top the waffles with the stewed cinnamon-sugar apples, and pour a little melted ghee over the top.

Tip: If you don't have a waffle maker, feel free to turn these into pancakes!

Apricot and Lavender Scones

This is a modern take on what my nanna would make every morning in her North Beach flat—hot black coffee and two toasted English muffins slathered in sweet apricot jam.

I took the essentials of her breakfast and turned it into a sweet apricot scone with a subtle aroma of lavender laced throughout. It's an unexpected flavor combination that somehow just works. Unlike many scone recipes, there is no kneading or waiting involved. Just bring the ingredients together, roll them into flat circles, dust with coconut sugar and then bake. Fifteen minutes later warm scones emerge from the oven, perfuming the kitchen with a floral sweetness.

MAKES 8–10 SCONES / V

1 flax egg (page 188)

2 cups (240 g) spelt flour

1 tbsp (12 g) baking powder

1 tsp dried lavender

¼ cup (50 g) coconut sugar, plus more for topping

6 tbsp (90 ml) coconut oil, cut into the flour

¼ cup (60 ml) almond milk

⅔ cup (160 ml) apricot conserve or jam

1 cup (150 g) dried apricots, chopped into fourths

Dollop of coconut yogurt or jam, optional for topping

Start by making the flax egg. Preheat your oven to 400°F (205°C) and line a baking pan. In a medium-sized mixing bowl, mix together the dry ingredients—spelt flour, baking powder, dried lavender and coconut sugar. Scoop out the coconut oil, and with a fork cut the coconut oil into the flour. I like to stop halfway through and use my hands to softly incorporate the oil into the flour by gently pinching the flour/oil into crumbly pieces. Once all of the oil has been incorporated into the flour, the batter should look a bit crumbly.

Now stir in the flax egg, almond milk, apricot conserve and dried apricots. Mix until just combined.

On a lined baking pan, form the scone batter into medium circles. I like mine large, about 4 tablespoons (30 g) of batter. Dust the top with coconut sugar and bake for about 18 to 20 minutes. Once cooked, let them cool for 5 minutes. Slice them open and add a dollop of coconut yogurt or jam to your scone for a delicious breakfast!

Tip: Using spelt flour makes for a heartier scone. If you want a more delicate scone, use a ratio of 1 cup (120 g) of spelt flour to 1 cup (100 g) of unbleached, all-purpose flour.

Morning Glory Bowl

I can't think of a more nourishing breakfast bowl than this one right here. Beautiful greens are sautéed until tender and sprinkled with creamy hemp seeds, avocado slices and fresh dill. It's a bowl that highlights the simplicity of flavor pairings between a few fresh herbs, spices and deep greens. When your morning calls for a breakfast that is undeniably delicious, while still packing in enough nutrients to cover breakfast and lunch, then this is definitely going to be the morning bowl you turn to.

Serves 3 / V, GF

1 tbsp (15 ml) coconut oil

½ small red onion, quartered and thinly sliced

½ fennel bulb, thinly sliced

2 cloves garlic, roughly chopped

1 tsp cumin powder

Pinch of chili flakes

Pinch of sea salt

2 cups (72 g) Swiss chard, stems removed, roughly chopped

1 cup (30 g) spinach

1 avocado, cut into fourths

2 tbsp (5 g) fresh dill

Small handful of cilantro

2 tbsp (20 g) hemp seeds

In a medium-sized saucepan, melt the coconut oil over medium heat. Add in the onions, fennel, garlic, cumin, chili and sea salt. Sauté for about 7 to 10 minutes, or until the onions are a bit translucent and have softened. If the bottom of the pan starts to dry out at any point, add a splash of water and mix all the ingredients together.

Now toss in the Swiss chard and spinach and sauté for another 7 to 10 minutes, or until the greens wilt down. Serve in bowls and add in the avocado slices, dill, cilantro, hemp seeds and another pinch of sea salt.

Juicy Baked Apples with Ginger-Coconut Cream

I live and die by the way of sweets. If you could tell me that eating sweets for every meal, or at least during every meal was acceptable, I would give up all other foods. Even bread.

I cannot, and will not, give up sweets. But I can certainly use healthier alternatives, like fruit, to coax out that sweet flavor. Roasting apples for nearly an hour caramelizes them and releases natural sugars. Stuff the apple with currants, nuts and maple syrup, and now we have a proper breakfast that walks the line of healthy, yet sweet.

SERVES 6 / V, GF

For the stuffed apple

6 apples (I use Fuji)

½ cup (75 g) raisins or currants

Big handful of walnuts (reserve a small scoop for extra topping), chopped

2 tbsp (30 ml) maple syrup

2 tsp (5 g) cinnamon powder

1 tsp vanilla powder or extract

½ tsp fresh ginger root, grated

Pinch of sea salt

2 tsp (10 ml) coconut oil, about ¼ tsp per apple

½ cup (60 ml) water

For the ginger-coconut cream

¾ cup (177 ml) coconut yogurt

¼ – ½ tsp fresh ginger root, grated

1–2 tsp maple syrup, depending how sweet you like it

Preheat your oven to 375°F (190°C). With an apple corer, take out a large portion of the apple core by carving a hole from the top of the apple to nearly the bottom— don't puncture the apple all the way through.

In a small mixing bowl, toss the raisins, walnuts, maple, cinnamon, vanilla, ginger and sea salt together.

Place the cored apples in a baking pan and stuff them with the mixture. Add a small amount of coconut oil to the top of each stuffed apple.

Add a few splashes of water directly on top of the stuffed apples and place them into the oven. Keep adding a splash of water to each apple every 10 minutes as it bakes— this keeps them moist. Cook the apples for about 40 to 45 minutes, or until they're soft and the skin is golden brown.

In the meantime, make the coconut cream by simply stirring all the ingredients together in a bowl.

Remove the apples from the oven and cool for 10 minutes. Top the apples with a sprinkling of extra nuts and serve each apple with a drizzle of the ginger-coconut cream.

Green Morning Smoothie

I was 24 years old, stuck in a work-life limbo, and I guess I was having what you might call an early quarter-life crisis. I quit my job, started a food blog and enrolled in night classes, all in the pursuit of getting a Masters in Nutrition. On that impulsive path, I signed up for an intensive 6-week, 7 a.m., all day long, all week long, summer chemistry course. This was the smoothie that accompanied me on those god-awful early morning drives down the peninsula.

When mornings are tight and you can't swing oatmeal or pancakes, this is the smoothie you want to have in your hand when walking out the door. It's loaded with the healthy breakfast essentials—almond milk, chia seeds, spinach, yogurt and banana—but with an unexpected pop of tropical flavor from the pineapple. That sweet taste was the highlight of those hectic morning drives. Quarter-life crisis or not, this smoothie reinforces that healthy breakfasts really don't need to take longer than 5 minutes.

SERVES 1 / V, GF

1 frozen banana, chopped

¾ cup (115 g) pineapple, chopped

¾ cup (177 ml) almond milk

¼" (5-mm) piece of fresh ginger root, peeled (optional, but it adds a great kick)

Handful of spinach leaves

1 tbsp (10 g) chia seeds

1 tbsp (12 g) flax meal or powder

1 heaping scoop of the yogurt of your choice

Place all the ingredients in a blender and blend on high speed until it is completely smooth and there are no banana or spinach pieces. Pour into a glass and enjoy immediately!

Tip: You can always make this smoothie the night before, seal it up in a mason jar and store it in your fridge for your morning breakfast. Just leave the chia seeds and flax out if you do this! They will clump together otherwise.

Honey-Poached Pears over Black-Sesame Granola and Yogurt

The first and last time I ever made an extravagant breakfast was when I was trying to impress a boyfriend by making cinnamon rolls from scratch. I should have tossed the recipe when I read that I needed to come home 12 hours later to roll out the dough. You see, I was 22, in college and 12 hours later meant leaving a party early on a Saturday night. Though the rolls did come out delicious, I ended up burning the face of my then-boyfriend when the hot icing slid off the bun and landed right on his chin, scarring it. With this recipe, there is no face burning or party exiting involved! To me, this is the fanciest sounding recipe: *honey-poached pears*. But in reality we're just relying on a pot of boiling water, cinnamon sticks and honey to cook a very impressive breakfast. After the pears have poached, sprinkle them with a generous handful of granola and a dollop of yogurt. Fancy breakfast done.

SERVES 2–4 / V, GF

For the poached pears

2½ cups (600 ml) water

2 Bosc or Bartlett pears, skin peeled

⅓ cup (80 ml) honey, or maple syrup if vegan

1 cinnamon stick

1 thumb of fresh ginger, thinly sliced

For the granola

1 cup (80 g) rolled oats

1 cup (120 g) oat flour

¾ cup (110 g) pistachios, chopped

¼ cup (40 g) black sesame seeds

Pinch of sea salt

3 tbsp (45 ml) coconut oil

3 tbsp (45 ml) honey, or maple syrup if vegan

3 tbsp (35 g) coconut sugar

Zest of 1 large orange

1 tsp fresh ginger root, grated, or ginger powder

1 cup (235 ml) yogurt of your choice

To make the poached pears, bring the water to a boil in a medium saucepan. Lower the heat to a simmer and add in the peeled pears, honey, cinnamon stick and ginger. Cook the pears for about 20 minutes, or until soft. After they've cooked, drain them of the honey water and let them cool down for a few minutes before slicing lengthwise to remove the core.

To make the granola, start by preheating the oven to 350°F (177°C) and line a baking pan with parchment paper. In a large bowl, mix the oats, oat flour, chopped pistachios, sesame seeds and sea salt. Now in a small saucepan on low heat, warm the coconut oil, honey, coconut sugar, orange zest and ginger for 1 minute. Pour this sauce onto the oat mixture and mix until everything is evenly coated.

Pour the granola on the lined baking pan. Firmly press the granola with your fingers to keep the batch compact. Bake for 15 to 17 minutes while turning the granola once halfway through. Make sure the edges are crisp but not burnt.

Remove from the oven and let cool for 10 minutes. Store in an airtight container (I use a mason jar) for up to a few weeks in your cupboard.

In a serving bowl, layer the yogurt, then the poached pear and top with a generous helping of granola.

Tip: Use coconut yogurt to make this meal completely vegan.

Raspberry-Fig Morning Bar

Back in the day I would consume fig bars as if they were candy. I would hoard and inhale packs of fig bars, and then discard all of the wrappers in a cabinet drawer that I thought my parents didn't know about. Well, they did and those mysteriously disappearing fig bars poured out of the cabinet, exposing my hijacking ways.

These raspberry-fig bars are a take on that childhood favorite. Yet, in this case, the bars are made from delicious, whole-food ingredients of fruity raspberries and chewy figs. Take the bars to go or enjoy with a cup of coffee or tea in the morning. Without a doubt, these are my new favorite breakfast bars.

MAKES 8–10 / V, GF

For the base

1½ cups (120 g) rolled oats

¾ cup (130 g) almonds

2 tbsp (30 ml) maple syrup

1 tsp cinnamon powder

1 tbsp (15 ml) coconut oil, melted

¼ cup (60 ml) almond milk

Pinch of sea salt

For the filling

1 cup (165 g) dried figs (cut off the hard stem on top if attached)

1 cup (150 g) fresh raspberries

1 tbsp (15 ml) maple syrup

¼ cup (60 ml) water

1 tbsp (15 g) arrowroot powder

For the topping

1 cup (80 g) rolled oats

1 tbsp (15 ml) maple syrup

½ tsp cinnamon

1½ tbsp (22 ml) coconut oil, melted

Pinch of sea salt

Start by making the base by preheating the oven to 350°F (177°C) and lining a small baking dish with parchment paper. Add all the base ingredients in the food processor and blend for about 20 seconds until part of the almonds have broken down and a solid batter has formed, sticking together. Press the batter into the lined baking dish, about ½-inch (13-mm) thick. Keep pressing into the dish until a solid, tight base forms. Bake for 7 minutes.

In the meantime, make the filling by roughly chopping the figs into small pieces, or add them into the food processor to chop for about 20 seconds (either method works). Now add all the filling ingredients, except the arrowroot powder, into a small saucepan and cook on medium-high heat for 5 minutes. Turn off the heat and then stir in the arrowroot and let rest for a few minutes.

While that's resting, make the topping by mixing all the topping ingredients together in a small bowl.

Assemble the bars by layering the raspberry filling evenly on top of the cooked base. Then add the topping over the filling, gently pressing down, covering the raspberry mixture below.

Bake for 25 to 30 minutes, or until the top is golden brown. Let cool for 10 minutes and slice into bars.

Creamy Cardamom and Date Porridge with Citrus Yogurt

Two things come to mind when I think of porridge: (1) late-night study sessions mulling over mind-numbing statistic notes and (2) the aroma of cinnamon enveloping the entire house while my college roommate prepared her morning porridge. She was the "OG" (original gangster) of meal preps. Every night back in 2011, she was whipping up porridge for the next morning's breakfast. She got me into real porridge and out of the instant oatmeal packs.

Five years later, I've tweaked her recipe and made an infusion of my own—spiced porridge with chopped sweet dates. But what makes this porridge unusually delightful is the dollop of citrus yogurt. The citrus balances the creaminess and adds a layer of freshness to the porridge. So now with this recipe comes two things: (1) a delicious breakfast and (2) a house that smells entirely of sweet cinnamon. That's a pretty good deal.

SERVES 1 / V, GF

1 cup (235 ml) almond milk

½ cup (40 g) rolled oats

2 tsp (10 ml) honey, or maple syrup if vegan

3 Medjool dates, pitted and roughly chopped

½ tsp cinnamon powder

⅛ tsp cardamom powder (optional)

½ tsp vanilla powder or extract

Zest of ½ the orange and juice from the entire orange

½ cup (120 ml) yogurt of your choice

Handful of pecans, roughly chopped

Start by preparing the porridge. In a medium saucepan on high heat, bring the almond milk, oats, honey, dates and all the spices to a boil. Then lower the heat to a simmer. Cook for 5 to 7 minutes, or until the oats have absorbed the almond milk and the dates have softened.

Now simply prepare the orange yogurt by mixing together the orange zest, juice and yogurt.

Add the porridge to a serving bowl, top with the orange yogurt and chopped pecans.

Tip: Use coconut yogurt to make this meal completely vegan.

Vanilla Spiced Strawberry Baked Oatmeal

This is a tried and true recipe. Every Sunday night my mom bakes variations of this oatmeal and packs them into little portions to last the entire workweek. This way breakfast is always taken care of. Unless I'm over at the house, in which case, I'll take bites out of every single container so it looks like none were disturbed … She always notices and later an annoyed call to my phone follows.

Keep in mind that this recipe is the basis for baked oatmeal. Get creative with it and add in any fruits, nuts, seeds or spices that you have lying around. Baked oatmeal is a very flexible and forgiving recipe. Usually any fruit and nut combo turns out a delicious breakfast.

SERVES 5 / V, GF

1½ cups (355 ml) hot water

2 cups (160 g) rolled oats

2 tbsp (20 g) chia seeds

3 tsp (7 g) cinnamon powder

2 tsp (10 ml) vanilla powder or extract

¾ cup (115 g) currants or raisins

2½ cups (375 g) ripe strawberries, cut into thin slices (¼" [6mm]-thick)

1½ cups (185 g) raspberries

2 ripe bananas, chopped

2 tbsp (30 ml) maple syrup

Handful of pecans, chopped

Zest of 1 small lemon

Pinch of sea salt

¾ cup (177 ml) almond milk

Start by preheating your oven to 350°F (177°C) and boiling the water. In a mixing bowl, add the oats and chia seeds, and pour the hot water on top. Let this sit until the oats have absorbed all the water, about 5 minutes.

In a separate mixing bowl, add all the spices, currants, all the fruit, maple, pecans, lemon zest, pinch of sea salt and mix well. To this bowl add the chia-oat mixture and almond milk. Mix very well so that all the berries and oats are coated in the almond milk.

Pour the batch evenly into a medium-sized baking dish and bake for 20 minutes. Feel free to reheat this the next morning until warm.

Coconut Chia Pudding with Strawberry-Rose Compote

You know those cafes that just feel like home? Like a *Cheers* episode where you walk through the door and everyone turns, beaming with toothy smiles. A spot where they *definitely* know your name. Okay, this might be an exaggeration at most places, but it's actually not too different from a cafe that I frequent. It is a true neighborhood establishment. The owner has even seen me mature from a sweets-aholic kid who always bought his organic gummy bears to a chocolate-selling young adult. This is the coconut chia pudding that I made for his cafe last year.

I know that many of the readers of my blog don't live in San Francisco, so I wanted to share this recipe. It's a breeze to make. Even though it sounds kind of fancy, there isn't much to it. The coconut chia pudding is covered with a lovely rose compote and topped off with a crunchy Black Sesame Granola (page 25). Just make sure to plan ahead for this recipe; it needs to sit for an hour, if not overnight. A great breakfast to enjoy at home or cozied up with a coffee at your second home ... that cafe where everyone knows your name.

Serves 2 / V, GF

For the chia pudding

1 cup (235 ml) full-fat coconut milk

1 cup (235 ml) coconut water

6 tbsp (60 g) chia seeds

1 tsp honey, or maple syrup if vegan (optional, since the coconut water is sweet on its own)

For the compote

1 apple, peeled and cut into bite-size cubes

1½ cups (225 g) strawberries (if frozen, run under warm water for 30 seconds to thaw)

1 tbsp (15 ml) water

¼ tsp rose water extract (if you don't have rose water, no worries, it will be a delicious strawberry compote instead)

1 tbsp (15 ml) honey, or maple syrup if vegan (optional)

1 tsp chia seeds

Black Sesame Granola (page 25)

To make the chia pudding, simply stir all the ingredients together and let this sit for at least an hour (stir after 30 minutes) or, even better, overnight. Keep in the refrigerator for up to 3 days.

For the compote, in a medium-sized saucepan, bring the apple, strawberries, water, rose water and honey to a boil. Lower the heat to medium-low and cover the saucepan with the lid ajar. Cook for 10 minutes, or until the fruit is tender. Add in the chia seeds at the end and stir well. Keep in the refrigerator in an airtight container for up to 3 days.

Serve the chia pudding with a few tablespoons of rose compote on top and a handful of the Black Sesame Granola. Enjoy!

Sweet Orange and Vanilla Bircher Muesli

Bircher muesli is essentially milk and oats left to soak overnight in the fridge. If I stopped here this probably wouldn't do much for you. Actually, you might be turned off. What you do need to know, more so than anything else with bircher muesli, is how to load it up with flavor! As with baked oatmeal, add in any spices or fruits you like. For this recipe, I got a little daring and squeezed in orange juice, vanilla and a ripe banana, almost mimicking the flavor of a Creamsicle. Another bonus with bircher muesli is that it doubles as a great on-the-go breakfast. Just make a large batch the night before and come morning you'll have a hearty breakfast, with even more muesli ready for the next few days.

SERVES 1 / V, GF

¾ cup (177 ml) almond milk

¼ cup (60 ml) fresh orange juice

½ cup (40 g) rolled oats

1 tbsp (10 g) chia seeds

½ ripe banana, mashed

¼ tsp vanilla powder

2 heaping (30 ml) tbsp yogurt of your choice, as topping

To prepare the bircher muesli, simply add all the ingredients into a medium bowl and mix well. Pop this into the refrigerator to set for at least an hour, or ideally overnight. Stir the bircher muesli, top with yogurt and seal it up in a mason jar to take with you to work, school or for a post-workout meal!

Tip: Use coconut yogurt to make this meal completely vegan.

Fruity Toast Parfait

This is exactly what you should do for those days when you open the fridge and surprise (!), all you have lying around is a piece of bread, yogurt, some fruit and maybe leftover granola—make an elegant clean-out-the-fridge breakfast toast.

Before I was in this situation I never would have thought to pair yogurt with bread. Doesn't sound too appealing. But toasted bread, layered with yogurt and then topped with juicy berries and crunchy granola, is a breakfast that I can get behind. Yet, what makes this toast so delicious is the fresh mint and drizzle of honey. Both add a sweetness that complements the fruity toast. This is what I like to call a last-minute toast parfait.

SERVES 1 / V

1 slice of sourdough toast

3 tbsp (45 ml) yogurt of your choice

Small handful of blackberries and blueberries

Small handful of Black Sesame Granola
(page 25)

1 tsp fresh mint leaves, chopped

Drizzle of honey, or maple syrup if vegan

Pinch of sea salt

This is a very simple breakfast. Layer the warm toast with yogurt, then the fresh berries, handful of granola, sprinkling of fresh mint, drizzle of honey and a pinch of sea salt.

Tip : Use coconut yogurt to make this meal completely vegan.

Savory Sweet Potato Nests

Remember when the spiralizer made its debut a few years ago and everyone lost their minds because did you ever consider that zucchinis could be swirled and turned into noodles? Or how about sweet potato noodles? Or even sweet potato nests? Nope, never. Yet, sweet potato nests have become a staple breakfast recipe of mine. Entangled sweet potato noodles are baked into crispy little nests that make for the perfect vehicle to be topped with anything you'd like. Some people crack an egg into a nest, while others add a whole slew of spices. I prefer to keep it simple with creamy avocado slices and radishes, and a light sweetness from cooked beets. This recipe just goes to show that breakfast can be innovative and delicious with a plate adorned with simple vegetables.

MAKES 4 NESTS / V, GF

1 medium-sized sweet potato

1 tbsp (15 ml) olive oil

Pinch of sea salt

2 small cooked beets, chopped into cubes

½ avocado, thinly sliced

1 radish, thinly sliced

Small handful fresh dill

Start by preheating the oven to 400°F (205°C). Now spiralize your sweet potato. If you don't have a spiralizer, use a potato peeler to ribbon the sweet potato and then cut it in half lengthwise into thinner slices that resemble noodles. Toss the noodles in a medium-sized bowl with the olive oil and sea salt and mix well. Divide the sweet potato noodles into fourths and place them on a baking pan in compact circles. Press firmly with your hands to create the compact circle—this is very important for making crispy nests. Bake for 23 to 25 minutes until the sides are crispy and golden brown.

Simply remove the nests from the oven and top each with equal amounts of the beets, avocado, radish, dill and a pinch of sea salt.

Yogurt Parfait with Homemade Lemon "Curd" and Coconut-Pecan Crunch

If anyone has reservations about healthy eating—let's say your friends or family—the best thing to do is never tell them from the get-go that what they're eating is healthy. Let's take this recipe for example: lemon "curd." Sounds pretty decadent, right? Well I would never say, "Hey, guess what guys? There's tofu inside!" That might scare the hell out of them. But unknown to them, tofu is actually what makes it creamy without having to use raw eggs. So postpone your reveal till after the fact and then witness a look of confusion mixed with pleasure. Unless you want the parfait all to yourself; in that case, also tell them there's arrowroot and turmeric inside. At this point they will be so confused about what they just ate … Enjoy!

Just make sure to plan ahead for this recipe; it needs to sit for an hour.

SERVES 2 / V, GF

For the lemon curd

4 tbsp (60 ml) ghee, or coconut oil if vegan (but ghee works slightly better)

¾ cup (190 g) organic silken tofu

⅓ cup (75 ml) honey, or maple syrup if vegan

Zest and juice of 3–4 small lemons (I like mine really lemony, so I go with 4)

2 tbsp (28 g) arrowroot powder

½ tsp vanilla powder (optional)

Pinch of turmeric powder (optional, but adds a nice yellow tint to the "curd" without adding any extra flavor)

For the coconut-pecan crunch

1 cup (120 g) pecans

½ cup (60 g) walnuts

2 tbsp (30 ml) ghee, or coconut oil if vegan

½ cup (35 g) unsweetened desiccated coconut shreds

½ cup (120 ml) maple syrup

1 tbsp (7 g) cinnamon

Sea salt

1 cup (235 ml) yogurt of your choice

To make the lemon curd, simply melt the ghee and then add all the lemon curd ingredients into the food processor or blender. Blend until the mixture is smooth and silky, about 1 minute. Let the lemon curd rest for at least an hour in the fridge. During this time the lemon curd will thicken slightly. Store the lemon curd in the fridge in an airtight container for up to a week.

To make the coconut-pecan crunch, preheat the oven to 350°F (177°C) and line a baking pan. Roughly chop the pecans and walnuts, and melt the ghee. Add the nuts into a mixing bowl and pour in the melted ghee, coconut, maple syrup and cinnamon. Make sure all the ingredients are well mixed. Pour the coconut-pecan mixture into the lined pan and press firmly with your fingers to keep the mixture compact, then sprinkle with sea salt. Bake for 13 minutes. Remove from the oven and let it cool for 10 minutes. Store in an airtight container for up to a few weeks in your cupboard.

When serving your parfait, simply take a bowl or a glass jar and layer first the yogurt, then a few tablespoons of the lemon curd and top it off with a small handful of the coconut-pecan crunch.

Tip: Use coconut yogurt to make this meal completely vegan.

Lemon Verbena and Mint Tea

About a year ago my family took my dad to dinner for a special birthday. To him every birthday is a milestone or just a great excuse to celebrate somewhere fancy. And we went somewhere *fancy*. Between the courses, I kept noticing that the server was carrying trays of petite Moroccan glasses filled with tea. All I can say is that the aroma was captivating—citrusy notes entangled with sweet, earthy ones. As it turns out, it was just a simple blend of fresh peppermint and lemon verbena leaves.

Serves 2 / V, GF

1 handful of fresh mint leaves

1 handful of fresh lemon verbena leaves

1½ cups (355 ml) hot water

Add the leaves to a pot of boiling hot water. Let the leaves steep for about 3 to 5 minutes. Remove the leaves and pour your tea into a cup to enjoy!

Tip : If you are having a hard time finding lemon verbena leaves or tea, simply use the peel of ½ a lemon in its place. But if you're interested in growing lemon verbena, it is actually a pretty easy garden plant, as is mint. If you enjoy this tea, I suggest looking into planting or potting mint and lemon verbena. Then you can enjoy this tea anytime you like!

Cozy Chai-Apple Cider

I'm in the business of planning my day around physical comfort. If you like taking long hot showers, wearing sweaters most days, cozying up to the 9 blankets on your bed and likely having a hot drink nearby, than I'd say you're with me on this concept. So when my cousin sent me a message suggesting that I might like to play around with a chai apple cider recipe, I sent back only a heart-eyed emoji, meaning, "yes." So here you have it, a warming blend of stewed apple juice, cinnamon sticks and chai tea. The perfect nightcap and addition to your 'physical comfort' repertoire.

Serves 2 / V, GF

1 cup (235 ml) apple cider

½–¾ cup (120–175 ml) water (depending on how sweet you like it)

1 chai tea teabag

½ cinnamon stick

Add all the ingredients into a saucepan and bring to a boil. Once it starts to boil, lower the heat to medium-low and warm for 5 minutes. Discard the cinnamon stick and teabag, pour into a mug and enjoy!

The Creamiest Nut Milk for Your Coffee—Macadamia-Almond Milk

For a solid three months, I was held up in Saint Frank's cafe in San Francisco because of *this* nut milk. In a city where healthy food reigns and everyone from ages 15 to 70 is in the same lululemon uniform with almond lattes in their hands, you'd think there'd be almond milk cafes opening up by the dozens. Well I've found only two. And when I came across Saint Frank's nut milk, a true obsession was born.

It's also the cafe where I reconnected with an old friend, bonded with a long-time one and opened an unassuming email that read: 8th and Lake Cookbook. So I am now under the impression that good things happen in the presence of this nut milk. It's luscious, it's creamy and you'll love it, I promise. Just make sure to plan ahead for this recipe; it needs to sit for four hours, if not overnight.

SERVES 3-4 CUPS / V, GF

1¼ cups (215 g) raw almonds

¾ cup (115 g) raw macadamia nuts

4 cups (950 ml) water

Pinch of sea salt

Place your almonds and macadamia nuts in a bowl along with enough water to cover the nuts. Set the bowl in the refrigerator overnight or for at least 4 hours. This will allow the nuts to soften—this is a very crucial step in having creamy nut milk. When the nuts are done soaking, drain the water and rinse well. Add the nuts to a blender along with the 4 cups of water, and blend for 1 to 2 minutes until the nuts have ground down into a crumble or paste. Be careful not to completely pulverize the nuts into the water. Now line a bowl with cheesecloth and slowly pour the nut milk through. Then squeeze the bottom of the cheesecloth, making sure you get every last drop of the delicious nut milk. Finally, seal the nut milk in an airtight container and store in the refrigerator for up to 3 to 4 days.

Enjoy this creamy nut milk in your coffee, tea, food or even on its own!

Tip: It's all in the macadamia-almond ratio. The macadamia nuts work to keep the milk creamy but go easy on them or you'll end up with a very nutty-flavored milk.

2

Living on the Vedge

Hearty vegan mains that meat lovers will dare to try.

During a weekend away from the city, I came up with a Cupboard Curry (page 50) recipe on the fly. I came home, made the recipe once more and gave a portion to my sister to try. Her husband, a 6'5" meat enthusiast, opened the fridge and saw the leftover curry. Poking at it to see if there were any bites of chicken underneath the layers of squash and eggplant, he called my sister to say, "Let me guess, this is one of Marie's creations?" She laughed it off. Well, when I saw him the very next day he told me this story and went on to express that he ended up loving the curry! And he is not a man of hyperbole or one who particularly likes vegetables. Yet, he concluded that the curry, in fact, did not need chicken and that he loved it as it was.

This is exactly the aim of this collection of recipes—to simply showcase the brilliance of well-cooked vegetables, to celebrate their vibrant flavors and to set aside the stigma that a meal is not yet complete with only a plate of veggies. The beauty is in how you cook and season vegetables. I, too, would pass on a bowl of steamed kale that resembles the blandness of baby food. But when you take that same kale, toss it into a pot to stew under a bath of creamy coconut milk and spiced tomatoes, then it is a proper meal. If you're cooking for a veggie novice, I'd go for the Three-Bean African Spiced Chili (page 62) because the warming spices and hearty portobello mushrooms mask the fact that it's completely plant-based. Yet, if you're after something fancier, Basil-Stuffed Zucchini Rolls (page 66) is right there for you. And for a tried and true favorite, I have yet to meet someone who isn't completely enthralled by Honey-Roasted Carrots and Fennel over Herby Lentil Salad (page 61).

Cupboard Curry

Earlier this year, I took a trip to visit my friend in San Luis Obispo for the week. Since people in SF will nearly ostracize you for food waste, I loaded up my car and took any perishables with me. One of the nights in SLO, there was a full-blown rainstorm: flooding, power outage and broken umbrellas littering the streets. We decided to eat in, and with everything I packed away, I made this exact curry. In my opinion, this is the epitome of healthy fast-food. Most of the ingredients are already in your cupboard and showcasing veggies in a hearty curry is a brilliant way of introducing a veggie-loaded meal to a meat lover. Diced tomatoes stew away in a bath of coconut milk, while the squash and zucchini cook down into tender pieces. Serve atop brown rice for a very delicious and cozy meal.

SERVES 5 / V, GF

¾ kabocha squash

2 tbsp (30 ml) olive oil

½ red onion, thinly sliced

3 cloves garlic, roughly chopped

Sea salt to taste

1 tsp cinnamon powder

1 tsp cumin powder

2 tsp (5 g) coriander powder

½–1 tsp chili powder (optional)

1 tsp turmeric powder

¼ tsp chili flakes

1 medium zucchini, cubed

¾ (28-oz [790-g]) can diced tomatoes

1 (14-oz [400-g]) can full-fat coconut milk

½ cup (120 ml) water

1 (14-oz [400-g]) can garbanzo beans, drained and rinsed

3 handfuls of spinach

Brown rice, for serving

Start by cubing the kabocha squash. Cut the top off the squash and cut it in half. Scoop out the insides and cut the squash into large bite-size pieces—similar to how you would cut slices of cantaloupe. And no need to peel the skin as it is completely edible and will soften after cooking.

In a large sauté pan over medium-high heat, warm the oil and add in the onions, garlic, sea salt and all the spices. Bring the heat back down to medium and let this cook for about 5 minutes, stirring occasionally. Add a few splashes of water if the bottom of the pan starts to dry out and mix well.

Add in the squash and zucchini, and turn the heat to high, cooking for another 5 minutes. Add the canned tomato and cook on high until it starts to boil. Then lower to medium and cook for another 5 minutes. Stir occasionally.

Now add in the coconut milk, extra water and garbanzo beans, and cook for another 15 minutes, or until the squash is tender.

Toss in the spinach and cook for a few more minutes, or until the spinach has wilted down.

Serve with brown rice and enjoy!

Zesty Beluga Lentils over Orange-Glazed Cauliflower Florets

Last year I was in L.A. for my birthday and my mom took me out to a great spot for dinner where we ended up having a restaurant-dream experience. If you're a germaphobe, you might want to stop here. When we arrived we were seated at one long table where everyone next to us, including another table down, all shared food! A whole bunch of us strangers swapped and traded dishes, shared stories and had a grand time.

One of those shared dishes involved citrusy veggies and another, roasted cauliflower. So I took the best of both and brought them together. Citrus-glazed cauliflower florets with lentils is a meal that will always remind me of what took place on that one beautiful L.A. night.

SERVES 3–4 / V, GF

1 cup (200 g) beluga lentils (black lentils)

1 cauliflower head

2 heaping tbsp (35 ml) olive oil

½ fennel bulb, quartered and thinly sliced

4 cloves garlic, roughly chopped

Sea salt

Juice of 2 medium-sized oranges, divided, and zest of 1 orange

1–2 tsp (3–6 g) chili flakes

2–3 tbsp (30–45 ml) red wine vinegar

Start by cooking the lentils as the box instructs and add ½ teaspoon of salt to the pot of water.

In the meantime, set your oven broiler to high, line a baking pan and remove the stem of the cauliflower head. Removing the stem lets the cauliflower break off into smaller florets. Cut the florets so that they're all similar in size—medium, bite-size pieces.

In a medium saucepan over medium-high heat, warm the olive oil for 1 minute. Now add in the cauliflower, fennel slices, garlic and sea salt. Sauté for about 10 minutes, stirring occasionally. If the pan ever dries out, add a few splashes of water and mix well. Now on a lined baking pan, add the sautéed veggies with a drizzle of olive oil and broil in the oven for 5 minutes.

Remove the veggies from the oven and toss the cauliflower mixture back into the saucepan. Add the juice from 1 orange, chili flakes, red wine vinegar and a few pinches of sea salt and mix well.

Now that the lentils have cooked and have absorbed all the liquid (if they haven't, just pour the excess liquid out), squeeze in the juice from 1 orange and its zest. Top the lentils with the cauliflower mixture (including any of the vinegar-juice that may be left over) and enjoy!

Tip: I like my cauliflower florets very spicy, so I opt for 2 teaspoons (6 g) of chili flakes, but try 1 teaspoon first and see if you'd like to add more spice.

Minty-Pistachio Falafels with Tzatziki Dip

The beauty of falafels is that one big batch will last you all week and then some. Wrap falafels into a collard green, pop them onto salads for extra heartiness, or enjoy them solo, dunked in creamy tzatziki dip.

MAKES 15–18 FALAFELS / V, GF

For the falafels

1 cup (150 g) pistachios

1 (14-oz [400-g]) can garbanzo beans, drained and rinsed

2 cloves garlic

2 small shallots or ½ small yellow onion

2 tbsp (30 ml) olive oil

2 tbsp (30 ml) water

1 tsp cumin powder

2 small handfuls of fresh mint leaves

2 small handfuls of fresh parsley leaves

Small squeeze of juice from half a lime

Pinch of sea salt

For the tzatziki

¾ cup (175 ml) yogurt of your choice

2 cloves garlic

Juice of half a lemon

1 tsp fresh dill

Pinch of sea salt

1 small cucumber, peeled and grated

2–4 collard leaves (optional, for wrap)

1 radish, sliced (optional, for salad)

1 avocado, sliced (optional, for salad)

1–2 cups (30–60 g) any greens (optional, for salad)

Start by preheating the oven to 375°F (190°C) and lining a baking sheet with parchment paper. Simply add all the ingredients for the falafels into a food processor. Pulse for 10 to 15 seconds until the chickpeas have broken down but are not completely blended—we do not want to turn the mixture into hummus. We're looking for a chunkier texture of pistachio and chickpeas, slightly mixed together.

Scoop out the falafel mixture with an ice cream scooper and place on the lined baking sheet (or use your hands to roll into small balls). Make sure the falafels are no bigger than 1½-inches (40-mm) thick; they should be on the smaller side. Bake for 18 to 20 minutes, or until the top is slightly golden brown and crispy, with a creamy center.

For the tzatziki, add all the ingredients, except the cucumber, into a food processor and pulse until well combined. Pour the tzatziki into a serving bowl and mix in the grated cucumber.

To enjoy the falafels as a wrap, lay the collard leaves on a cutting board and use a knife to shave down the stem, making it easier to fold and eat. Dollop a few teaspoons of the tzatziki near the middle of each leaf, fill each leaf with a few falafels and wrap the leaves as you would a burrito. Cut each collard wrap in half.

To enjoy the falafels in a salad, simply choose your greens, add a few radishes and avocado slices and drizzle the tzatziki over the top, creating a creamy dressing. Enjoy!

Tip: Since these falafels are baked, they will be a bit more crumbly than deep-fried falafels. Be delicate when handling them after they have baked. Also, use plain coconut yogurt to make this meal completely vegan.

Baked Sweet Potato with Harissa Roasted Tomatoes

Baked sweet potatoes will forever remind me of that one night in Amsterdam when we uncovered the code to a secret bar, ditched it for a spot that lit drinks on fire and finished the night in a mermaid-dolphin lounge right before getting locked out of our four-lock door apartment … in the rain.

Before that night commenced, we went out for dinner. On the menu were stuffed sweet potatoes. This is an elevated take on that dish with a spicy roasted tomato spread beneath crispy sweet potatoes, black beans, toasted pumpkin seeds and avocado slices.

SERVES 3 / V, GF

For the harissa roasted tomatoes

1 pint cherry tomatoes (about 2 cups [300 g])

4 cloves garlic, peeled

1 tsp harissa

Sea salt to taste

For the sweet potato and toppings

3 small sweet potatoes

¾ cup (150 g) black beans, warmed

⅓ cup (45 g) thinly sliced red onion, cut in half

1 avocado, sliced

Handful of pumpkin seeds

Handful of microgreens (optional topping)

Start making the harissa roasted tomatoes by roasting your cherry tomatoes and garlic cloves. Preheat your oven to 400°F (205°C). Wrap the cloves of garlic in foil and place them on a lined baking dish along with the cherry tomatoes and bake for 25 minutes, or until the skins of the tomatoes have slightly blistered and the juices have burst through the sides.

Once the tomatoes have cooked, remove them and the garlic from the oven and let cool for 10 minutes.

In the meantime, turn up the heat to 420°F (215°C) and line another baking sheet. Prick the sweet potatoes a few times with a fork and toss them onto the lined baking sheet. Cook the sweet potatoes for 40 to 50 minutes (depending on the size), until the skin is crispy and the inside is tender.

As the sweet potatoes cook, add the tomatoes, garlic, harissa and salt into a food processor and pulse for 10 seconds until the tomatoes have broken down and everything is well mixed. Taste the sauce and see if you would like to add more harissa.

Once the sweet potatoes have finished cooking, it's time to assemble your plate! Add a layer of the harissa roasted tomato sauce onto the plate, top with the sliced roasted sweet potato and sprinkle with black beans, red onion slices, avocado, pumpkin seeds, microgreens and a drizzle more of the harissa roasted tomato sauce.

Spicy Chana Masala

This is a quintessential weeknight meal for me. Chana Masala is a beautiful dish that brings home the idea that a few spices can completely shape a meal. Take an unassuming can of beans, let it simmer in a rich tomato stew with a myriad of spices, and just like that, you have a deliciously cozy meal to warm up to.

SERVES 3–4 / V, GF

2 tbsp (30 ml) coconut oil

1 medium yellow onion, cut into quarters and thinly sliced

Dash of chili flakes

1 tsp cumin powder

2 tsp (5 g) coriander powder

1 tsp garam masala (very spicy, but if you don't have this on hand use ½ tsp of chili powder)

½ tsp turmeric

Sea salt to taste

3 cloves garlic, grated

Small knob of ginger root, grated

1 (14-oz [400-g]) can chickpeas, drained and rinsed

1 cup (150 g) green beans, cut in half with stems removed

1 (14-oz [400-g]) can diced tomatoes

Juice of half a lemon, plus more for topping

½ cup (120 ml) water

Brown rice, for serving

Handful of fresh cilantro

In a large sauté pan over medium-high heat, melt the coconut oil and add in the thinly sliced onions, all the spices and sea salt. Bring the heat down to medium and sauté for about 10 minutes, stirring occasionally. Add a few splashes of water if the bottom of the pan starts to dry out and mix well.

Now add in the grated garlic and ginger, chickpeas, green beans, canned tomatoes, lemon juice and water, and cook for another 25 to 30 minutes, or until the tomato sauce reduces and the beans have absorbed the spicy flavor. Stir occasionally.

Serve the chana masala over brown rice and top with fresh cilantro and an extra drizzle of lemon juice.

Honey-Roasted Carrots and Fennel over Herby Lentil Salad

There is one particular lentil salad available at Peet's Coffee that my mom and I just crave. It's one of those things that you'd oddly go out of your way for, and if they don't have it, it pretty much ruins your day. And one day that happened. I guess I'm not the only one who appreciates this salad …

Black lentils are mixed with fresh mint and parsley, and tossed with red wine vinegar—wrapping the salad in a subtle sweetness. To make this salad a meal without the inclusion of meat or seafood, roast up some rosemary-honeyed carrots and throw in a few dates for crispy bites of caramelized sweetness. This is one of my favorite dishes to serve to friends who might not be sold on the plant-based eating experience. It's a food rainbow, highlighting how delicious a plate full of veggies can taste when roasted with an array of fresh herbs and served alongside black lentils.

SERVES 3–4 / V, GF

For the honeyed carrots

6 medium-sized carrots

1 fennel bulb, quartered

1 tbsp (15 ml) olive oil

1 sprig of rosemary leaves

Pinch of sea salt

1 tsp honey, or maple syrup if vegan

4 Medjool dates, pitted and roughly chopped

For the lentil salad

1 cup (200 g) beluga lentils (black lentils)

5 tbsp (12 g) fresh parsley, roughly chopped

5 tbsp (12 g) fresh mint leaves, roughly chopped

⅓ cup (45 g) red onion, very thinly diced

1 red bell pepper, very thinly diced

2 tbsp (30 ml) olive oil

1 tbsp (15 ml) honey, or maple syrup if vegan

3–4 tbsp (45–60 ml) red wine vinegar

Pinch of sea salt

Start by roasting the carrots and fennel. Preheat the oven to 425°F (218°C) and line a baking tray with parchment paper. In a mixing bowl, add in all the ingredients, except the honey and dates, and mix well. Lay the veggies flat on the baking tray. Cook for 35 minutes. Remove the tray from the oven and drizzle the honey over the roasted veggies and toss in the dates. Cook for another 5 to 10 minutes, or until tender.

Now prepare the lentils by cooking them as instructed on the box and add in a teaspoon of salt to the pot of water. Once the lentils have cooked and have absorbed all the liquid (if they haven't, just pour the excess liquid out), stir in all the remaining lentil salad ingredients.

To serve, plate the lentils first and top with the roasted veggies and dates.

Three-Bean African Spiced Chili

I got the idea for this recipe from a friend who tried African chili years ago. Essentially, it's a laundry list of warming spices simmering away with fennel and onions, and then stewed alongside beans, hearty portobello mushrooms and squash. It's an incredibly satisfying version of classic chili and I have yet to meet someone who isn't enchanted by it, even die-hard meat eaters. Generous chunks of portobello mushrooms bulk up the chili, making it into a complete meal. This is a perfect choice for anyone who is venturing into the world of plant-based eating.

SERVES 4 / V, GF

2 tbsp (30 ml) olive oil

1 small yellow onion, quartered and thinly sliced

1 fennel bulb, quartered and thinly sliced

4 cloves garlic, roughly chopped

1 cinnamon stick

1 tsp coconut sugar

1 tsp cinnamon powder

1 tsp turmeric powder

1 tsp ginger powder

1 tsp coriander powder

Sea salt to taste

1 tbsp (15 g) tomato paste

1 large tomato, roughly chopped

3 cups (720 ml) low-sodium vegetable broth

1 medium delicata squash or sweet potato, cubed (you can leave the skin on)

1 red bell pepper, roughly chopped

1 cup (16 g) fresh cilantro, roughly chopped

1 cup (150 g) canned black beans, drained and rinsed

1 cup (250 g) canned black-eyed peas or kidney beans, drained and rinsed

1 cup (250 g) canned cranberry beans, drained and rinsed

1½ cups (115 g) portobello mushrooms, cut into big chunks

In a large sauté pot (I like to use a Dutch oven) over high heat, warm the olive oil and add in the sliced onions, fennel, garlic, cinnamon stick, coconut sugar, all the spices and sea salt. Bring the heat down to medium and sauté for about 10 minutes, stirring occasionally. Add a few splashes of water if the bottom of the pan starys to dry out and mix well.

Add in the tomato paste and the chopped tomato and mix well. Now add in the broth, cubed delicata, bell pepper and cilantro. Bring the pot to a boil and then turn it down to a simmer. Cook for about 10 to 15 minutes.

Now add in the beans and portobello mushrooms to the chili and bring to a boil. Once it's boiling, reduce it to a simmer and cook for about 10 minutes until the veggies and mushrooms are tender and the chili sauce has reduced down and thickened.

Remove the cinnamon stick and serve the chili in a bowl, or seal it up in a mason jar and bring it with you for lunch on-the-go!

Tip: If you cannot find black-eyed peas or cranberry beans, feel free to use more black or kidney beans.

Veggie-Filled Miso To Go

Miso is my soup of choice with or without a cold. Miso paste is a powerful flavor bomb. It is both hearty and salty, and a little goes a long way. Mix together with tender carrots, zucchinis, bok choy and tofu for a veggie-packed soup filled with the makings of a hearty meal, sans the addition of meat or fish. You can make it in bulk, or pack it into large mason jars and add hot water to the seasoning, bringing the soup to life at your choosing. Now you can have your soup on demand, just like your shows.

MAKES 2 (16-OZ [450-ML]) MASON JARS / V, GF

2 mushrooms, thinly sliced (I use cremini mushrooms)

1 small carrot, ribboned with a potato peeler

1 small zucchini, ribboned and then sliced in half lengthwise

1 bok choy head, chopped into fourths

Small handful of extra firm organic tofu, cubed (per jar)

2 – 2½ tsp (10 – 13 g) white miso paste (per jar)

¼ – ½ sheet of nori, depending on how much you like the flavor of seaweed (per jar)

¼ tsp ginger root (per jar), grated

½ tsp tamari (per jar) (gluten-free soy sauce)

1 tbsp (10 g) green onions, chopped (per jar)

Pinch of chili flakes

Hard-boiled egg, cut in half (optional)

16 oz (450 ml) hot water (per jar)

Start by steaming all your sliced veggies. Place your sliced veggies into a steamer basket and cook for about 3 minutes, until tender. If you don't have a steamer, use a medium-sized sauté pan with a thin layer of water, enough to cover the bottom of the pan. Add in all the veggies and cover with a lid. Cook on medium-high heat for about 3 minutes. If the water evaporates at any point, add a splash more to prevent the veggies from burning.

In the meantime, add the tofu, miso, nori, ginger, tamari, green onions and chili flakes to both mason jars (or any 16-ounce [450-ml]) jar). Once the veggies have cooked, portion out the veggies to half per jar and seal with the lid. Keep the jars in the fridge until you're ready to eat that night or the next day.

When you are ready, add boiling hot water to the veggie-filled jars, seal with the lid and shake very well, mixing all the flavors together. Place a towel around the glass jar as you shake, making sure not to burn your hands—it can be quite hot. Take the lid off and make sure the miso paste is totally incorporated. If not, use any utensil to push the miso around the sides, breaking it up. Now add in the hard-boiled egg and enjoy your miso soup on the go!

Tip: If you're bringing this to work for lunch (which I strongly suggest!), store the jar in the office fridge and come lunch time, add hot water from the water cooler or tea kettle, and mix well!

Basil-Stuffed Zucchini Rolls (Involtini)

This was the absolute last recipe that I created for this cookbook, which I am okay with. Had I created it early on, this is the one meal that would have populated my Instagram feed and my belly. It is absolutely delicious and tastes as if there is more to it than there really is. A hearty basil filling is coiled between crispy zucchinis and layered atop stewed garlic tomatoes. It's a beauty. Enjoy, my friend.

SERVES 4 (1 SET OF ROLLED ZUCCHINIS PER PERSON) / V, GF

For the rolls and filling

4 large zucchinis, stems removed

4 tbsp (59 ml) olive oil, divided

Sea salt

⅔ cup (16 g) fresh basil leaves

1 (7-oz [200-g]) block of firm organic tofu

Zest and juice of ½ of a large lemon

3 tbsp (30 g) nutritional yeast

3 cloves garlic

2½ tbsp (20 g) capers

For the tomato sauce

1 (14-oz [400-g]) can tomato sauce

2 cloves garlic, grated

Handful of basil leaves

Start by roasting the zucchini. Preheat your oven to 420°F (215°C) and line a baking sheet (you may have to use two baking sheets). Slice the zucchinis lengthwise into ¼-inch (6-mm) thick strips. Lay them flat on the lined baking sheet and drizzle 2 tablespoons (30 ml) of the olive oil and sea salt over the top. Cook in the oven for 10 minutes. Then remove from the oven and flip each zucchini slice over, cooking the opposite side for another 10 minutes.

While these cook, make the filling. Simply add the remaining filling ingredients (including the last 2 tablespoons [30 ml] of olive oil) into a food processor and pulse until well combined, about 15 seconds. The filling should be smooth in texture, mimicking ricotta cheese. Set this aside until the zucchinis are done cooking.

While the zucchini slices are cooling down, make the tomato sauce. Set aside two 9-inch (23-cm) round baking dishes. Mix the tomato sauce, garlic and basil into a bowl. Now pour the tomato sauce into the two baking dishes, filling the bottom with a thin layer of sauce.

To make the rolls, place about 2 teaspoons (8 g) of filling at one end of the zucchini slice. Roll each slice into tight coils and place cut-side down into the tomato sauce. Drizzle the zucchinis with olive oil and a sprinkle of salt. Pop both dishes into the oven and cook for 25 minutes, or until the sauce reduces and the tops of the rolls are golden brown.

Tip: Nutritional yeast can be found at health food stores or online. It is very inexpensive.

3

Not Looking for Commitment? 30-Minute Meals.

Speedy recipes for when you only have time for your Netflix queue.

For the modern, twenty-first-century individual who juggles work, school, family life and/or daily workout routines on top of a *very* demanding Netflix lineup, these recipes are for you.

I can be pretty lazy in the kitchen; any recipe that takes longer than 35 minutes feels taxing, which is why I completely rally behind the "30-Minute Meal" sentiment. These recipes focus on speedy meals that can be thrown together on the fly, while coaxing the delicious flavors from each ingredient. Moroccan-Inspired Eggplant and Okra Tagine over Lemony Quinoa (page 70) is a hearty stew that can be made in bulk and enjoyed the next day—shortening another night of cooking. Or for something a bit more exotic, the Tropical "Sushi" Rolls with Macadamia Nuts and a Sesame-Miso Dip (page 82) is another delicious option. The variety of meals that can be whipped up in less time than it takes to watch an episode of *Game of Thrones* is endless.

Moroccan-Inspired Eggplant and Okra Tagine over Lemony Quinoa

The first time I enjoyed a traditional tagine was after I booked a $30 flight to Morocco, hiked for three days in the scorching heat in a panic from fear of falling off the cliffs to my death, while a donkey hiked briskly ahead, carrying on its back all the ingredients for tagine. Untraditional, I know. I took the cooking tips I learned from my Moroccan hiking guide, came back to the States and made this tagine. Loaded with Morcoccan spices, eggplant and okra, this is similar to the delicious tagine that nearly served as my final meal on earth.

SERVES 3-4 / V, GF

For the lemony quinoa

1 cup (210 g) white quinoa

Sea salt

Zest of 1 lemon and juice of ½ that lemon

For the okra tagine

1 tbsp (15 ml) coconut oil

1 large yellow onion, quartered and thinly sliced

2 cloves garlic, roughly chopped

1 tsp cumin powder

½ tsp cinnamon powder

½ tsp ginger powder

¼ tsp turmeric powder

¼ tsp clove powder (optional)

Pinch of chili flakes

Sea salt to taste

1 cup (235 ml) water

2 cups (160 g) eggplant, cubed

1 tbsp (15 g) tomato paste

1 (14-oz [400-g]) can of diced tomatoes

1½ cups (120 g) okra, cut in half

Handful of parsley

Handful of pine nuts (optional)

Start by cooking the quinoa by following the instructions on the box. Add in a ½ teaspoon of salt to the pot of water. Once the quinoa has fully cooked, stir in the lemon zest and lemon juice.

In a large sauté pan over medium-high heat, melt the coconut oil and add in the onions, garlic and all the spices. Bring the heat back down to medium and let this cook for about 5 minutes, stirring occasionally. If the bottom of the pan dries out at any point, add a few splashes of water and mix everything together.

Add in the water and cubed eggplant and cook for another 10 minutes, or until the eggplant softens, stirring every so often.

Add in the tomato paste, canned tomatoes and okra, and cook for another 10 to 15 minutes, until the eggplant and okra are tender and the tomatoes have cooked down.

Serve the okra tagine over the quinoa and top with fresh parsley and pine nuts.

Travel + Food Tip: I was living in Italy when I decided to travel to Morocco, hence the cheap flight, and I booked the ticket through either Ryanair or Easy Jet airline. Also, if you can't find okra, swap in zucchini in its place.

Caramelized Fennel and Dill Cakes

One of my girlfriends and I used to meet at a park during lunch to brainstorm the ways in which we were going to start a business together, becoming the next Oprah and Gayle. The ideas that we thought had legs involved mini polenta cakes, a pressed almond milk factory and finally, a coconut yogurt business. None stuck. But at least I get to use the polenta cake concept here!

This is a particularly fun dish to make if you're out to impress someone, as they are beautiful and look fancy. Yet, it's all an illusion since only polenta, a few toppings, and a sauté pan are needed here. These cakes are sautéed until golden and then paired with caramelized fennel and herbs. At least a few great recipes came from our entrepreneurial expeditions.

MAKES 4 SLICES / V, GF

3 tbsp (45 ml) olive oil, divided

1 medium fennel bulb, quartered and sliced

Pinch of sea salt

1 tbsp (15 ml) maple syrup

2 tsp (2 g) green onions, chopped into thin rings

2 tsp (2 g) dill, chopped

4 (½" [13-mm]-thick) slices of precooked polenta roll

2 tbsp (15 g) any flour (use brown rice flour as a gluten-free option), reserved for the polenta

In a medium-sized sauté pan on medium-high heat, warm half of the olive oil for 1 minute. Add in the fennel slices and a pinch of sea salt, and sauté for about 5 to 7 minutes, until the fennel is tender but still crisp. Remove from the heat and add in the maple syrup, green onions and dill. Mix well.

Remove the fennel mixture and set aside while you add in the remaining olive oil to the sauté pan. As the oil warms on medium-high heat, lightly press the polenta into the flour, so that it coats each side. This will prevent the polenta from sticking when cooking in the oil. Now sauté the polenta slices for 3 to 5 minutes on each side, until they're crisp and slightly golden brown. Remove from the sauté pan and pat the polenta with a paper towel to remove any excess olive oil.

Top each polenta cake with the sweet fennel mixture and enjoy!

> *Tip:* I would suggest using a precooked polenta roll. It saves so much time and there are plenty of brands that offer polentas rolls with no additional flavoring added. I found mine at Trader Joe's, but Amazon has them as well! Just type in "precooked polenta roll or tub."

Sweet Ricotta-Sage Cakes

This is my "impress anyone and everyone" recipe. When I think, "What is an easy meal that requires very little maintenance in the kitchen?" this comes to mind every single time. My friends love it. I love it and I have yet to encounter a person who doesn't want to devour these mini polenta cakes the moment they're placed in front of their face. Creamy polenta slices are lathered in ricotta and topped with crispy pears. Add a drizzle of honey and a sprinkling of fresh sage for a flavor profile that teeters on sweet yet savory. Enjoy solo or pair it with the Caramelized Fennel and Dill Cakes (page 73) for a meal that I know all who surround you will enjoy.

MAKES 4 SLICES / V, GF

2 tbsp (30 ml) olive oil

4 (½" [13-mm]-thick) slices of precooked polenta roll

2 tbsp (15 g) any flour (use brown rice flour as a gluten-free option), reserved for the polenta

4 tbsp (30 g) ricotta, or use coconut yogurt or vegan "cheese" if vegan

1 crisp Asian pear, or crispy apple, sliced thin

2 tsp (2 g) fresh sage leaves, chopped

Small handful of pistachios, chopped

Drizzle of honey, or maple syrup if vegan

Sea salt

Warm the olive oil in a medium sauté pan over medium-high heat. As the oil warms, lightly press the polenta into the flour, so that it coats each side. This will prevent the polenta from sticking when cooking in the oil. Now sauté the polenta slices for 3 to 5 minutes on each side, until they're crisp and slightly golden brown. Remove from the sauté pan and pat the polenta with a paper towel to remove any excess olive oil.

Assemble the polenta cake by first layering 1 tablespoon (7 g) of ricotta to each cake, then add four thin slices of pear, a sprinkling of fresh sage and pistachio and top it off with a generous drizzle of honey and pinch of sea salt.

Tip: Use coconut yogurt or vegan "cheese" instead of ricotta to make this meal completely vegan.

Spicy Garlic Noodles

Talk about a dish that brings back memories of studying abroad! Friends would come by after a late night at the Italian *discoteca* for this pasta. I wish I could tell you that this recipe was passed down on a handwritten note by my late Italian grandpa, but nope—it was most certainly a 2 a.m. food craving. It's a versatile recipe, too. I am happy to say that it has now made the transition from late-night food to a humble dinnertime meal. It's a punchy one, playing off the spicy chili flakes with a touch of sweetness from the sautéed garlic.

If you plan ahead, try it out with fresh pasta; this is by far the best way to enjoy it—lighter on the stomach and even quicker to cook up.

Serves 1-2 / V, GF

⅓ pound (150 g) fresh spaghetti of your choice (or dry pasta)

3 tbsp (45 ml) extra virgin olive oil

4 big cloves garlic, roughly chopped

½ tsp chili flakes or more, depending on how spicy you like it

Sea salt

Nutritional yeast, optional

Bring a large pot of salted water (about 1 tablespoon [15 ml]) to a rolling boil. Add in the spaghetti and cook as the package instructs.

In the meantime, warm the olive oil in a medium-sized sauté pan over medium heat for a minute. Bring the heat down to low and add in the garlic and chili flakes. Let this warm for about 3 minutes but be careful not to burn the garlic. Remove from the heat.

Once the pasta has cooked, drain it and then add the noodles to the garlic-chili oil. Mix well. Let the pasta cool down for about 5 minutes and then serve in bowls with a generous sprinkling of sea salt. You can also top with nutritional yeast for a cheesy bite!

Tip : Use a brown rice pasta for a gluten-free option.

Tahini Veggie Stir-Fry

As I was writing the introduction for this recipe, I got a text from a friend asking for a recipe from the cookbook that she could make for dinner. She also asked, "Yeah, but is it easy … ?" Immediately, I wrote back "EASSSSYYYY." I like it all to be quick and easy. To drive the point home, I despised cooking for most my life. Don't get me started on washing dishes. Cooking leads to dishwashing, so I drew the line right there.

What you need for this recipe is one pot for the veggies and one pot for the noodles. Cook up the noodles, then the veggies and toss it all together in a creamy tahini sauce. And if you're still not persuaded to make this for dinner tonight, well, let me just tell you that my friend wrote back, expressing that her and her Canadian bacon-eating boyfriend loved the stir-fry! It just goes to show that a creamy sauce, hearty soba noodles and a rainbow of veggies can convince any carnivore to venture to the plant-based side and thoroughly enjoy it.

Serves 2 / V, GF

For the tahini sauce

3 tbsp (45 ml) tahini

Juice of 1 small lemon

1 tbsp (15 ml) maple syrup

1 tbsp (15 ml) tamari (gluten-free soy sauce)

⅓ cup (75 ml) full-fat coconut milk

For the stir-fry

2 tbsp (30 ml) olive oil

Pinch of chili flakes

3 cloves garlic, roughly chopped

1 cup (340 g) red cabbage, shredded

1 medium carrot, ribboned with a potato peeler

2 medium zucchinis, ribboned and then sliced in half lengthwise

1 cup (150 g) sugar snap peas or snow peas, cut into thirds

2 handfuls of kale leaves, roughly chopped

1 tbsp (15 ml) water

Sea salt

⅓ packet of soba noodles (GF buckwheat noodles)

2 green onion stalks, chopped

Start by making the tahini sauce. Simply add everything into a blender or food processor and blend until creamy. Pour into a bowl and set aside.

Now bring a large pot of water to boil with 1 teaspoon of salt to prepare for the soba noodles.

As you wait for the water to boil, cook the stir-fry. In a large sauté pan on medium-high heat, warm the olive oil, chili flakes and garlic. After a minute, toss in all the veggies, water and sea salt and cover with the lid. Cook for about 5 minutes, stirring often.

Now cook the soba noodles as the box instructs, stirring often, as they tend to stick together.

Add a few tablespoons of the tahini sauce to the stir-fry, mix well, and cook for another 3 minutes, or until the veggies are tender but still have a crunchy bite.

Once the soba noodles have cooked, drain the water and immediately pour the noodles into the stir-fry. Top with the green onions and mix in a few more tablespoons of the tahini sauce. Serve the stir-fry in bowls and enjoy!

Carrot Ginger Soup

For those nights when lounging on the sofa sounds more appealing than cooking in the kitchen, here is a soup that will make cooking worthwhile. Sweet carrots are quickly sautéed and tossed into a blender with a handful of cashews. With a flick of a switch, the blender does all the work. Five minutes later you have a velvety soup that is slightly sweet and packed with a spicy curry kick. This is a soup to keep on rotation for when a speedy meal is needed and enjoyed in the company of a good TV series or classic book.

SERVES 4 / V, GF

4 medium carrots, cut into thin circles

4 cloves garlic, roughly chopped

¼ cup (35 g) yellow onion, roughly chopped

Pinch of sea salt

2 cups (480 ml) low-sodium vegetable stock

½ knob of a small piece ginger root, skin peeled

3 handfuls of cashew nuts

1 big tbsp (15 g) curry powder

¼ tsp turmeric powder

3 tbsp (45 ml) tamari (gluten-free soy sauce)

2 tbsp (30 ml) olive oil, plus more for topping

Juice of 1 small lemon

Small handful of pumpkin seeds, for topping

Smoked Gouda or vegan "cheese," for topping (optional)

In a medium-sized saucepan over high heat, add enough water to cover the carrots, garlic and onions, and bring to a boil. Once boiling, lower the heat to medium and add a pinch of sea salt and cook for about 8 minutes, until the vegetables have softened but are not fully cooked. Be sure to not let the pan dry out. If it does, add a bit more water. Once cooked, drain the water if there is excess in the pan and set the veggies aside.

There are a few ways to do the next part of blending the ingredients into a pureed soup. You can either use a very powerful high-speed blender, such as a Vitamix, or an immersion blender.

When using the high-speed blender method, simply add the carrot and onion mixture (without the water) to the blender, along with the rest of the ingredients. Blend until the broth turns creamy and warm. This should take at least 5 minutes on the high-speed or soup setting.

If you're using an immersion blender, transfer your carrot and onion mixture (without the water) to a large pot and then add in the remaining ingredients. Heat the pot until the soup is warm. Then blend the soup into a puree with the immersion blender.

Serve the soup and top with a drizzle of olive oil and pumpkin seeds. If you're a fan of cheese, add a little smoked Gouda or vegan "cheese" as well!

> *Tip:* If you're using a blender that is not high-speed, check the manual to see if it will allow for warm foods to be blended together. If it is not capable of this, then try adding all the ingredients into the blender, and blend until it is smooth and creamy. Then add the puree into a pot and heat until the soup is warm.
> Also, go easy on the ginger root—it is very powerful! If you want more ginger, you can always add a bit more after you've tasted it.

Tropical "Sushi" Rolls with Macadamia Nuts and a Sesame-Miso Dip

There is a funky little farmers' market cafe a block from the beach on Maui. It is a quintessential island-style hippie establishment with everything you'd want to eat. What drew me back to this cafe was the freshly rolled "sushi." Each one is wrapped with crispy veggies, avocado, crunchy macadamia nuts and is accompanied by a sesame-miso dip—nothing short of addictive. This version is a reincarnation of those rolls. It's a straightforward recipe with a few twists—I'm talking about that sesame-miso dip. It's an essential addition to the rolls and creates a tropical feel. A dipping sauce of tamari just won't cut it for these rolls.

MAKES 3—4 ROLLS / V, GF

For the sushi

1 cup (210 g) black or brown rice

⅓ (15-oz [425-g]) block of organic extra firm tofu

Splash of tamari (gluten-free soy sauce)

½ cup (170 g) carrots, shredded

½ cup (170 g) purple cabbage, shredded

3—4 nori sheets

½ avocado, thinly sliced lengthwise

Handful of macadamia nuts, chopped

Sea salt

For the sesame-miso sauce

1 tsp white miso paste

Juice of ½ small lemon

1 tbsp (15 ml) honey, or maple syrup if vegan

1 tsp black sesame seeds

¼ tsp peeled and grated fresh ginger root

1 tbsp (15 ml) olive oil

Start with cooking the rice by following the instructions on the box. Add 1 teaspoon of salt to the pot of water.

In the meantime, cut the tofu into ¼-inch (6-mm) strips lengthwise and mix them in a small bowl with a few splashes of tamari to coat the tofu. In a medium-sized sauté pan on medium heat, toss in the tofu and cook until the strips are crispy on each side, about 1 to 3 minutes. Remove the tofu from the pan and cut the strips into small cubes.

Now, shred the carrots and cabbage with a cheese grater (using the medium-sized hole) and mix them together.

Once the rice has cooked, prepare for the rolls. Lay 1 nori sheet onto a cutting board, shiny side down. With damp hands, spread a thin layer of rice over the nori sheet, leaving a 1-inch (2.5-cm) border along the edge of the nori that is farthest from you. At that border, dampen the edges—this is what seals the nori once it's finished being rolled.

Add a small amount of each sushi roll ingredient horizontally across the rice at the border closest to you. Gently pick up the edge of the nori sheet closest to you and tightly roll the veggies toward the opposite side. Continue rolling until the nori sheet covers the rice and seal the damp edge around the wrapped roll. With a sharp, wet knife, cut the roll into about 3 to 4 small pieces. Repeat until you are out of nori or stuffing.

To prepare the dipping sauce, simply mix all the ingredients together in a small bowl. Serve with the sushi rolls and enjoy!

Tip: White miso is generally pretty easy to find at health food or Asian grocery stores, but if you're having trouble finding it, you can always purchase it on Amazon.

Dinner Toast—Sicilian Caponata

The fate of a good caponata rests on the balance of sweet and sour. Eggplants sauté into tender bites and then are warmed in a sweet and sour stew of balsamic, currants, olives and capers. Yet, too many capers can quickly turn caponata into an overly salty affair, while an aggressive sprinkling of currants makes it cloyingly sweet. Nonetheless, this is a simple dish that just rests on the harmony of contrasting flavors. Once everything cooks down, scoop the delicious caponata onto a warm slice of sourdough for a speedy dinner.

SERVES 3-4 / V

4 tbsp (60 ml) olive oil, divided

1 large (about 3 cups [480 g]) eggplant, cubed into small pieces

Pinch of sea salt

½ small red onion, quartered and thinly sliced

2 cloves garlic, roughly chopped

⅔ cup (110 g) canned diced tomatoes

1 tbsp (15 ml) balsamic vinegar

1 tsp dried oregano

1 tbsp (2 g) fresh mint leaves, roughly chopped, plus more for topping

2 tbsp (4 g) fresh parsley, roughly chopped, plus more for topping

1 tbsp (12 g) coconut sugar

¼ cup (60 ml) water

1–2 tsp (3–6 g) capers

Pinch of chili flakes

Small handful of dried currants

Small handful of kalamata olives, roughly chopped

Small handful of pine nuts

3–4 slices of sourdough bread

Warm half the olive oil in a medium-sized sauté pan over medium-high heat for 1 minute. Add in the cubed eggplant, sea salt and a few tablespoons of water. Cook on medium for 5 to 7 minutes. If the pan ever dries out, add a few splashes of water and mix everything together again. Remove the eggplant from the sauté pan and set aside.

Add in the remaining olive oil to the same pan and on medium heat cook the onions, garlic and sea salt for 5 minutes. Stir occasionally. Now add in the tomatoes, balsamic, oregano, mint, parsley and coconut sugar, and stir well. Cook this for another 5 minutes.

Now add in the sautéed eggplant, water, capers, chili flakes, currants, olives and pine nuts, and cook for another 10 minutes, or until the eggplant is completely tender. Stir occasionally.

Remove the caponata and set aside. Add the slices of sourdough to the same sauté pan and warm both sides, collecting the delicious caponata flavor.

Place the toast on a plate and top it with the caponata and fresh parsley and mint.

> *Tip:* If there is one ingredient that is a must for this dish, it's the currants. The pops of sweetness in the caponata heavily rely on the currants, so try not to skip this ingredient.

4

Ex-Rated

Pizza, pasta and pants unbuttoned kind of night.

The Italians do it right. Skip over their unparalleled achievements in the arts, literature, fashion, film, smooth-talking, etc., and we get to the two achievements that *really* make a global impact—pasta and pizza. When I lived in Italy, I met an Italian man and what he said to me with the most expressive of hands, in broken English, was something I'll never forget, "Marie-*a*, I am-*a* on a diet now. So you see-*a*, I need to minimalize my-*a* pasta intake to two bowls a day." Two bowls? TWO bowls a day?! How much pasta can one man eat for *that* to be their diet? I stopped myself there because what that Italian man just touched on was a brilliant concept. Yes, perhaps minimize certain foods, but never fully cut out something that you truly love. For him it is pasta and for me it is sweets. I'm sure we all have something that we could enjoy more of in moderation during the day. Food should never be about deprivation. Sure, minimize what you will, but what would a life be without the joys of pasta and pizza every now and again? Clearly the Italians do not want to find out and I'm with them on that.

This chapter reframes traditional pasta and pizza recipes into ones of plant-based inclusion. I view both as blank slates. Choose any vegetable that you'd like, roast or sauté them in a medley of spices and herbs, and then pile all those delicious flavors atop a welcoming bed of pizza or pasta. Instead of cutting these favorites out of your diet, embrace these culinary masterpieces and get creative with the endless food pairings they license. Start with the Crispy Kale and Pesto Pizza (page 88) and then follow it up with the Sweet Winter Squash and Fennel Pizza (page 91) adorned with juicy pomegranate seeds. Or go for a warming bowl of Veggie Orecchiette in Brodo (page 92). *Buon appetito!*

Crispy Kale and Pesto Pizza on Chickpea Crust

There's a spot across the Golden Gate Bridge near a hiking destination that serves kale pizza on sourdough crust. It was one of the first places where I experienced an approach to pizza that excluded the usual toppings of sausage or pepperoni. Instead, they put some crispy kale leaves on top and laced it with a vibrant pesto sauce. It was divine, and is still the exclusive reason I hike so often. But after recreating this pizza using chickpea flour, keeping it light and healthy, I'm pretty sure my weekends just got a bit lazier. Now you and I can make this pizza anytime, anywhere … sans a hike.

SERVES 2 / V, GF

For the pizza crust

1 cup (120 g) chickpea flour (also labeled garbanzo bean flour)

1 tbsp (15 ml) olive oil, plus 1 tbsp (15 ml) for baking

1 tbsp (15 ml) almond milk

2 tbsp (30 ml) water

Generous pinch of sea salt

For the topping

1½ cups (100 g) kale leaves, stems removed

Squeeze of lemon juice

2 tbsp (35 g) ricotta, or vegan "cheese"

Chili flakes

Sea salt

For the pesto

1½ cups (40 g) basil leaves

1 tbsp (15 ml) lemon juice

4 tbsp (60 ml) olive oil

Small handful of pine nuts (or any nut)

4 cloves garlic

Sea salt (at least ½ tsp)

Start by making the chickpea pizza crust. Preheat the oven to 400°F (205°C). In a medium-sized mixing bowl, add in all the ingredients for the crust. Mix well with your fingers and knead the dough for about 5 minutes. The dough will start to come together and slightly resemble Silly Putty in texture. Now let the dough rest for 10 minutes.

While the dough is resting, prepare the kale. In a small bowl, toss the kale with a squeeze of lemon. Using your hands, gently massage the kale leaves. This helps to soften the leaves. After a few minutes of massaging, take a paper towel and squeeze the kale leaves, rubbing off any excess water or lemon juice. We want the leaves to be dry when we bake them, making the leaves crispier.

When you're ready to roll out the chickpea dough, line a cutting board with parchment paper and dust with a small handful of chickpea flour. Lay the dough on the parchment paper and with the help of a rolling pin (or perhaps a wine bottle), roll out the dough into a circle that is ¼-inch (6-mm) thick. Rub the top of the dough with 1 tablespoon (15 ml) of olive oil. Place the pizza onto a lined baking tray and pop into the oven to cook for 7 minutes.

In the meantime, make your pesto by blending all the ingredients in a food processor or blender and mix until smooth.

Remove the pizza from the oven and spoon about 3 tablespoons (45 ml) of the pesto evenly on top. Spoon the ricotta across the pizza as well and then top with the kale leaves. Drizzle with olive oil, chili flakes and a pinch of sea salt.

Now turn your oven broiler on high and once it's set, place your pesto-kale pizza into the oven on the rack furthest away from the broiler and cook for 3 to 4 minutes until the edges of the pizza are crispy and golden brown.

Remove from the oven, slice into pieces and enjoy!

Sweet Winter Squash and Fennel Pizza on Chickpea Crust

I'm all for a savory pizza but if one can slide its way into the sweet territory, I'll make it go there. This pizza is a nice in-betweener. Hearty winter squash is roasted into tender bites and layered onto a crispy pizza crust made from chickpea flour. With a drizzle of honey and pomegranate seeds, this pizza plays both sides. It's a great one to follow up a pizza filled with savory goodness.

Serves 2 / V, GF

For the toppings

1 cup (150 g) any winter squash (I like using delicata, acorn or kabocha squash), thinly sliced

1 fennel bulb, quartered and very thinly sliced

2 tbsp (30 ml) olive oil, divided

Sea salt

¼ cup (30 g) red onion, quartered and thinly sliced

Small handful of pine nuts

Sprinkle of goat cheese, or vegan "cheese"

Drizzle of honey, or maple syrup if vegan

Sprinkle of pomegranate seeds (optional, but I love its juiciness)

For the pizza crust

1 cup (120 g) chickpea flour (also labeled garbanzo bean flour)

1 tbsp (15 ml) olive oil, plus 1 tbsp (15 ml) for baking

1 tbsp (15 ml) almond milk

2 tbsp (30 ml) water

Generous pinch of sea salt

Start by roasting the squash. Preheat the oven to 420°F (215°C) and line a baking sheet. Cut the top off the squash and cut it in half. Scoop out the seeds and cut the squash into very thin, ¼-inch (6-mm) thick slices—similar to how you would cut slices of a cantaloupe but much thinner. And no need to peel the skin as it is completely edible and will soften after cooking. Place the squash onto the lined baking sheet and drizzle with olive oil and sea salt. Pop this into the oven and cook for 15 to 20 minutes, or until the squash is slightly crispy on the outside but not entirely cooked.

In the meantime, sauté the fennel in a medium-sized sauté pan on medium-high heat with a tablespoon (15 ml) of olive oil, sea salt and a splash of water for 5 to 10 minutes, or until slightly caramelized and golden in color.

Now prepare the chickpea pizza crust. In a medium-sized mixing bowl, combine all the ingredients for the crust. Mix well with your fingers and knead the dough for about 5 minutes. The dough will start to come together and slightly resemble Silly Putty in texture. Now let the dough rest for 10 minutes.

Once the squash has finished cooking, lower the oven heat to 400°F (205°C) and line a baking sheet with parchment paper. When you're ready to roll out the chickpea dough, line a cutting board with parchment paper and dust with a small handful of chickpea flour. Lay the dough on the parchment paper and with the help of a rolling pin (or perhaps a wine bottle), roll out the dough into a circle that is ¼-inch (6-mm) thick. Rub the top of the dough with 1 tablespoon (15 ml) olive oil. Place the crust on the lined baking tray and pop into the oven to cook for 7 minutes.

Remove the crust from the oven and top with the sautéed fennel, roasted squash, onions, pine nuts, goat cheese, honey and olive oil.

Now turn your oven broiler on high and once it's set, place your sweet winter squash pizza into the oven on the rack farthest away from the broiler and cook for 3 to 4 more minutes.

Remove from the oven, top with the pomegranate seeds for another burst of juicy sweetness and enjoy!

Veggie Orecchiette in Brodo

I am always surprised to find that in most cities there is virtually no cafe dedicated to homemade soup. There have been way too many nights when all I've wanted is a steaming bowl and I was left staring at the wall, thinking to myself, "Where can I go for homemade soup?" Yet, no place comes to mind. For some reason, there is no true soup establishment. If I were an investor, I'd say that this is a very untapped market.

So during those days of soup deprivation I make this orecchiette in *brodo* ("broth" in Italian). The beauty of this soup rests in its simplicity. No meat is needed to create a scrumptious meal that highlights a few modest greens simmering in broth. Thinly sliced leeks caramelize, creating an earthy base for the veggie stock. Tender peas hide within the crevasses of the pasta, revealing a burst of flavor with every spoonful. It's a delicious meal that comes together quicker than a trip to the market for a premade soup. This recipe is a welcomed alternative.

SERVES 2 / V, GF

¼ pound (113 g) orecchiette pasta or your favorite pasta shapes

2 tbsp (30 ml) olive oil

1 leek

3 cloves garlic, roughly chopped

Pinch of chili flakes

Sea salt to taste

2 cups (475 ml) low-sodium vegetable broth

2 cups (300 g) broccolini, cut lengthwise into thin strips

½ cup (75 g) frozen peas

1 tsp garlic powder

Handful of fresh parsley, roughly chopped

Squeeze of lemon

Parmesan cheese, or vegan "cheese"

Bring a large pot of salted water (about 1 tablespoon [15 ml]) to a rolling boil. Add in the pasta and cook as the box instructs.

In the meantime, warm the olive oil in a medium-sized sauté pan over medium-high heat for 1 minute. Remove the green stem portion of the leek and discard (or save for when you're making homemade veggie stock). Slice the leek in half lengthwise and cut into thin, half-moon rings. Bring the heat down to medium-low and add in the leeks, garlic, chili flakes and sea salt. Sauté for 10 minutes. If the pan ever dries out, add a few splashes of veggie broth and mix well.

Turn the heat to high and add in the veggie broth, broccolini and peas to the sauté pan. Once it starts to boil, bring the heat down to a simmer and cook for 5 to 10 minutes, or until the broccolini is tender but slightly crunchy. Right after it's done cooking, stir in the garlic powder.

Drain the pasta once it's cooked and add it to the sauté pan with the veggies. Mix well.

Serve in bowls with a sprinkling of parsley, a squeeze of lemon juice and parmesan cheese or vegan "cheese" if you'd like!

Tip: Choose brown rice pasta for a gluten-free option.

One-Pan Pasta with Crispy Brussels Sprouts

I squealed like a twelve-year-old fan girl at an 'NSYNC concert when I tasted this recipe. It has *everything* that makes for great pasta. Plus it's made in one pan. You know what that means … no real clean up! Toss the pasta into a pan with all the fixings, add boiling water and out comes tender noodles swimming in a delicious tomato sauce. Top it off with crispy Brussels sprouts for a wildly hearty meal. It just goes to show that pasta can be utterly delicious without the addition of meat, when it is instead filled with savory olives, capers, kale and basil.

SERVES 3–4 / V, GF

For the brussels sprouts

10 Brussels sprouts, sliced in half

1 tbsp (15 ml) olive oil

Sea salt

For the pasta

½ pound (230 g) pasta shape of your choice

1 (14-oz [400-g]) can tomato sauce

2 tbsp (30 ml) olive oil, divided

Zest of 1 small lemon

2 cloves garlic, roughly chopped

Pinch of chili flakes

1½ tbsp (15 g) capers

2 handfuls of kalamata olives, sliced in half

2 cups (475 ml) boiling water

3 cups (200 g) kale leaves, stems removed

Handful of fresh basil

Pinch of sea salt, for topping

Start by roasting the Brussels sprouts. Preheat the oven to 400°F (205°C) and line a baking sheet. Place the chopped Brussels sprouts on the baking sheet and drizzle with olive oil and sea salt. Pop into the oven and cook for 35 minutes, or until the sprouts are golden and crispy.

About halfway through cooking the Brussels sprouts, start preparing the pasta. In a large sauté pan, add every ingredient for the pasta (including the boiled water), except the kale leaves and basil, and bring to a boil on high heat. Cover with a lid and stir often so that the pasta doesn't stick together. After about 5 minutes of cooking, lower the heat to medium and stir in the kale and basil, and continue cooking until the pasta is cooked through and has absorbed enough liquid.

Top the finished pasta with the crispy Brussels sprouts, an extra drizzle of olive oil and pinch of sea salt.

Tip: Choose brown rice pasta for a gluten-free option.

Simple Orzo Pasta with Roasted Tomatoes, Olives and Basil

At the first signs of a sunny forecast, San Franciscans flock to the beach. Pale bodies dot the sand and groups of millennials blast what seems to be the *exact same* playlist while an afternoon of debauchery ensues.

My sister, her husband and I join the rest of the city at the beach for a tamer picnic. When I bring fruit, they bring orzo pasta salad. When they offer me a bite, I come at it full force. It is so very good. And since I'd like to have this pasta more than five times a year, I've made my own. Roasted tomatoes burst across the orzo, smothering the tiny pasta in a delightful sweetness. Liberally sprinkle this with fresh basil and a squeeze of lemon juice.

SERVES 3–4 / V, GF

2 cups (300 g) cherry tomatoes

4 tbsp (60 ml) olive oil, divided

Sea salt to taste

½ pound (230 g) gluten-free orzo pasta of your choice

⅓ cup (60 g) kalamata olives, chopped

1 cup (25 g) fresh basil, chopped

Juice of 1 small lemon

4 tbsp (30 g) feta, goat cheese, or vegan "cheese"

Small handful of toasted pine nuts (optional)

Start by roasting the tomatoes. Preheat the oven to 400°F (205°C) and add the tomatoes to a lined baking pan. Drizzle with 1 tablespoon (15 ml) of olive oil and sea salt. Mix well. Pop them into the oven to cook for 20 minutes, or until the skin has blistered and the tomato has softened.

Bring a large pot of salted water (about 1 tablespoon [15 ml]) to a rolling boil. Add the pasta and cook according to the instructions on the box.

Before you drain your pasta, reserve about 2 tablespoons (30 ml) of the pasta water. Drain the pasta and then immediately toss it in a large mixing bowl with the reserved pasta water and 2 tablespoons (30 ml) of olive oil. Mix well because this is what helps the orzo not stick together. Toss in all the remaining ingredients, including the roasted tomatoes and the last tablespoon (15 ml) of olive oil, to the pasta and mix again. When you pour in the tomatoes, also pour in all of the juices from cooking—this is delicious and helps to flavor the orzo. Taste the orzo to see if you'd like to add more lemon juice, basil, sea salt, etc. Serve warm or cold!

Tip : As this pasta comes together with just a few ingredients, a drizzle of high-quality extra virgin olive oil is a nice touch, elevating the flavors while adding a note of fruitiness.

5

Bento Boxes and Buddha Bowls

What to do with allll those leftovers.

The act of a two-year-old playing "chef" in a plastic kitchen set-up, flailing plastic fruit around, pairing bacon with strawberries and eggplant with chocolate, is eerily similar to that of preparing bento boxes and Buddha bowls. Take that same approach, plus the creative freedom of a preschooler, and apply it to your bowls! Bring everything out from the back of your fridge, toss it together with a generous drizzle of dressing and there you have it—a complete meal that celebrates all the ingredients that were on their last legs.

The practicality of these bowls, coupled with the mixing and matching of foods, creates endless meal opportunities. I've also included four dressings to jump start your bowl experimentations. If you have some crispy sweet potato wedges left over, add them to a bowl of massaged kale, pickled onions and olives, and top it off with an herby yogurt dressing. Or, take the last scoop of pesto and slather it between bites of crispy snow peas and asparagus. This style of meal is salvation for those nearly departed leftovers that you may have no idea what to do with.

Modern Japanese Bento Box

The idea of a Japanese bento box is so appealing. Take already cooked foods, tuck them nicely into a portable lunch box and your next meal is set. A classic bento box generally holds room for rice, fish/meat, fruit and vegetables, making it an incredibly flexible concept. Adding a generous helping of roasted squash and black rice negates the need for meat, instead creating a delicious veggie-rich bento box that is ridiculously satisfying.

Usually my M.O. is to make large batches of black rice, steamed greens, savory squash and sesame-carrot salad, and portion them out for the week. But this is just an example of the foods I enjoy mixed together. Make what excites you or even cook these recipes individually and enjoy them as a side dish.

SERVES 2–3 / V, GF

For the roasted squash

½ kabocha squash or any winter squash

1 tbsp (15 ml) tamari (gluten-free soy sauce)

1 tsp olive oil

1 tsp coconut sugar

Pinch of sea salt

For the black rice and kale

1 cup (210 g) black rice

1 tsp tamari (gluten-free soy sauce), plus ½ tsp

3 cups (200 g) kale leaves, stems removed

¼ – ½ tsp garlic powder

For the sesame-carrot salad

3 medium carrots, shredded

⅔ cup (225 g) red cabbage, shredded

2 tbsp (20 g) sesame seeds

2 tbsp (30 ml) maple syrup

2 tbsp (30 ml) lemon juice

1 nori sheet, chopped, for topping (optional)

Start by roasting your squash by preheating the oven to 420°F (215°C) and lining a baking sheet. Cut the top off the squash and cut it in half. Scoop out the seeds and cut the squash into large bite-size pieces—similar to how you would cut slices of a cantaloupe. No need to peel the skin as it is completely edible and will soften when cooked.

In a medium-sized mixing bowl, toss together all the ingredients for the squash and place them evenly on a lined baking sheet. Roast for 30 to 35 minutes, or until the squash is tender and golden brown. Remember to flip the squash in the oven at 15 minutes.

While the squash cooks, make the rice. Cook the rice as the box instructs and add 1 teaspoon of tamari to the pot as well. Once cooked, set aside to cool.

As the rice cooks, simply steam the kale leaves. In a medium-sized sauté pan, add a thin layer of water, enough to cover the bottom of the pan. Add the kale, garlic powder and ½ teaspoon of tamari, and cover with the lid. Steam on medium heat for about 5 minutes, or until the kale has wilted down. If the water evaporates at any point, add a splash to prevent the kale from burning.

Finally, toss all the ingredients for the sesame-carrot salad into a bowl and set aside.

Assemble your bowl by adding as much of each ingredient as you'd like. Store the rest in an airtight container in the fridge for another meal later in the week!

Tip : Use the medium side of a cheese grater to easily shred the carrots and cabbage. Also, feel free to make any part of this recipe on its own for another dish!

Peppery Arugula Salad with Warm Winter Squash and Farro

This is another example of great flavor combinations for your next bento box. It's also a recipe that I was shackled to, but in a good way (is there a good way to be shackled?). This bowl simply has it all. Speckles of farro stick to avocado slices for each delicious bite that is creamy yet nutty. And then comes the crispy squash entangled in peppery arugula leaves. Each bite sings with flavors, textures and hearty veggies, showcasing the power of a plate piled high with delicious whole foods. No meat needed here.

SERVES 2 / V

For the salad

½ cup (90 g) farro or barley

½ tsp sea salt

½ any winter squash (I like delicata or kambocha for this recipe)

2 tbsp (30 ml) olive oil, reserved for squash

1 avocado, cubed

Small handful of macadamia nuts, roughly chopped

2–3 large handfuls of arugula

For the honey-Dijon dressing

1 tbsp (15 g) whole-grain Dijon mustard

1 tbsp (15 ml) lemon juice

1 tsp honey, or maple syrup if vegan

3 tbsp (45 ml) olive oil

Splash of water

Pinch of sea salt

Start by cooking the farro by following the instructions on the box. Add ½ teaspoon of salt to the pot of water.

In the meantime, roast the squash. Start by preheating the oven to 420°F (215°C) and lining a baking sheet. Slice the squash lengthwise down the center. Remove the seeds and pulp, and cut the squash into thin half-moon rings. Drizzle the olive oil and sea salt over the squash, and mix well. Place the squash on the lined baking sheet and cook for 35 to 40 minutes, turning the squash halfway through.

Once the squash has cooked, add it to a mixing bowl along with the avocado, cooked farro, macadamia nuts and arugula.

For the dressing, simply mix all the ingredients together in a small bowl. Pour the dressing over the salad and mix well.

Sautéed Collard Greens with Sautéed Tofu and Spicy Black-Eyed Peas

One of my friends took a trip to Portland, Oregon, came back and announced that she had the most *amazing* sautéed veggie bowl of her life. With such a proclamation coming from a seasoned vegetarian, of course I asked for the recipe … in detail. What she took from that meal were three high points: (1) collard greens (2) tofu (3) and black-eyed peas. So I began with that, adding a few greens, some beans and tofu to a hot pan of sautéed, crispy garlic and ginger. Top it off with a generous squeeze of Sriracha and this is what I like to call a modern fast-food experience: a vegetarian-forward meal that comes together in minutes that is loaded with flavor and won't break the bank.

SERVES 2 / V, GF

1 tbsp (15 ml) sesame oil, or coconut oil

2 cloves garlic, grated

1 small knob of ginger, peeled and grated

½–1 tsp chili flakes (I like mine spicy so I go all the way at 1 tsp)

1 tbsp (12 g) coconut sugar

3–4 tbsp (45–60 ml) tamari (gluten-free soy sauce)

4 cups (270 g) collard greens, with stems removed

3 tbsp (45 ml) water

½ (15-oz [400-g]) block of extra-firm organic silken tofu

⅔ cup (110 g) cooked black-eyed peas beans, or black beans

Sriracha

In a medium sauté pan on high heat, warm the oil for 1 minute. Then add in the garlic, ginger, chili flakes, coconut sugar, tamari and mix well. Now lower the heat to medium and toss in the collard greens and water and mix well, coating the collard greens in the spices. Cook for about 5 minutes.

Then add in the tofu and beans. Cook for 5 more minutes, or until the greens have softened and the tofu and beans are warm.

Serve in a bowl with a squeeze of Sriracha and enjoy!

Greek-Inspired Kale Salad with Roasted Sweet Potatoes and Herby Yogurt Dressing

If you have friends who question the praise of kale (maybe they've only experienced it steamed without seasoning or raw without being massaged with dressing), I completely side with them. Instead of eating kale straight from the ground, massage it between your hands with lemon juice for a minute. This helps to soften the kale leaves instead of leaving them in a raw state that resembles bark. Now, make the salad even better by embellishing it with roasted sweet potato slices, tangy pickled onions and olives and a drizzle of herby dressing. This, I'm sure, is a kale salad that will persuade non-kale enthusiasts otherwise.

SERVES 1 / V, GF

For the salad

3 kalamata olives

A few pickled onions

Small handful of walnuts

3 cups (200 g) massaged kale (see Tip below), stems removed

½ medium-sized roasted sweet potato

Small handful of pea shoots or microgreens (optional)

For the yogurt and dill dressing

¼ cup (60 ml) Greek yogurt

1 tbsp (15 ml) lemon juice

1–2 tbsp (15–30 ml) olive oil

½ tsp clove garlic, grated

1 tsp fresh dill, roughly chopped

Pinch of sea salt

For the salad, roughly chop the kalamata olives, pickled onions and walnuts, and toss them into a mixing bowl, along with the chopped massaged kale leaves (see Tip below). Cut the roasted sweet potato into thin, circular pieces and add to the bowl as well.

Make the dressing by simply mixing all the ingredients together in a small bowl. The dressing makes 2 to 3 servings. Add about 1 tablespoon (15 ml) of dressing to the salad and then see if you'd like another dollop.

Tip: If your kale is very stiff, try the massaged kale method. All you have to do is squeeze a teaspoon or so of lemon juice onto the kale and then massage the kale leaves with your hands for a few minutes. This process helps to soften the leaves, making the kale easier to chew and digest.

Also, you can use plain coconut yogurt to make this meal completely vegan.

Golden Beet Salad with Lemony Butter-Bean Hummus

I'm under the impression that salads taste better when hummus is involved. And since hummus is creamy, it nearly blankets the salad in dressing when mixed well. Fun fact: Did you know that you could use any bean to make hummus? Not just garbanzo (which is the general default), but butter beans, black beans and even lentils! Hummus is an impressive condiment.

This recipe calls for butter beans, which are creamier than garbanzo beans, to enhance the dressing aspect of the dish. For aesthetic purposes when I cook for friends, I first dollop the hummus into the middle of the salad and then ask them to mix it well. While the hummus works as the dressing, a nice squeeze of lemon finishes off the salad on a fresh note.

SERVES 1 / V, GF

For the salad

¼ cup (40 g) fennel, thinly sliced

1 small radish, thinly sliced

2 cups (200 g) massaged kale (see Tip below), stems removed

1 golden beet, cooked and cubed into quarters (red beets work too)

Small handful of pumpkin seeds

Sea salt

Drizzle olive oil and lemon juice, for topping

For the hummus

1 (14-oz [400-g]) can butter beans

2 cloves garlic

2 tbsp (30 ml) tahini

Zest of 1 lemon, plus juice of 2 lemons

2 tbsp (30 ml) olive oil

1 tbsp (15 ml) water

½ tsp salt

For the salad, slice the fennel and radishes into very thin slices and toss all the salad ingredients into one mixing bowl. If you have a mandolin tool, use this to slice the vegetables, but if not, just slice them as thinly as you can.

For the hummus, first drain and rinse the beans. Then add all the ingredients into a food processor and blend until whipped and creamy. Taste the hummus and see if you'd like to add more lemon juice or salt.

Add a little squeeze of lemon juice and drizzle of olive oil over the salad and mix together. Then place a large dollop of the hummus onto the salad. I love to mix the hummus around the salad to act as a creamy dressing. Seal the rest of the hummus in an airtight container and pop it into the fridge for up to a few days.

Tip: If your kale is very stiff, try the massaged kale method. All you have to do is squeeze a teaspoon or so of lemon juice onto the kale and then massage the kale leaves with your hands for a few minutes. This process helps to soften the leaves, making the kale easier to chew and digest.

Crunchy Asparagus and Snow-Pea Quinoa Bowl with Arugula Pesto

This recipe pretty much sums up the idea of a Buddha bowl. And if you're asking "Why is it called a Buddha bowl?" Well, I honestly have no idea, but I guess we can Google that later … but after we make this bowl.

It is simple—steam a whole bunch of veggies until crispy, not cooked. Then, smother them in a peppery arugula pesto. And that, my friend, is how you use up all your leftover veggies and pesto, and turn them into a Buddha bowl. If you're serving this to a meat lover, go heavy on the pesto and nutty quinoa, bulking up the salad into one incredibly delightful meal.

SERVES 3–4 / V, GF

For the salad

½ cup (110 g) black quinoa or black rice

½ bunch of asparagus

2 small carrots

½ cup (75 g) snow peas or sugar snap peas, cut in half

⅓ cup (50 g) frozen peas

½ tsp sea salt

Handful of hazelnuts, chopped, for topping (optional)

For the arugula pesto

1 cup (115 g) walnuts

3 tbsp (45 ml) olive oil

3 cups (60 g) arugula

1 cup (30 g) spinach

Juice of 1 lemon

2 tbsp (30 ml) water

Sea salt

Start by cooking the quinoa by following the instructions on the box. Add in a ½ teaspoon of salt to the pot of water.

In the meantime, prepare the veggies for steaming. Cut the bottoms off the asparagus and discard. Keep the tops of the asparagus and then slice each stem into thirds at an angle (as in photo). Cut the rest of the veggies in this manner, except the frozen peas.

Add the asparagus, carrots, snow peas, frozen peas and ½ teaspoon of salt to a medium-sized sauté pan on high heat and fill the pan with just enough water to cover the veggies. After the water starts to boil, cook for 3 minutes. Fill a bowl with cold water and put the veggies in to stop them from cooking. This process of blanching keeps the veggies vibrant in color and crisp in texture. The veggies rest in the cold-water bath until the quinoa has finished cooking and then are drained.

As the quinoa cooks, make the pesto. Start by placing only the walnuts and olive oil into the food processor and blend for about 25 seconds. Breaking down the nuts first makes for a very creamy pesto. Then add in the rest of the ingredients and blend until smooth. Taste the pesto to see if you'd like to add more salt or lemon juice.

Once the quinoa has cooked, add a few scoops to a serving bowl and mix in half of the veggies with a few dollops of the pesto. Mix well so that the pesto coats all the veggies. Top with the chopped hazelnuts and enjoy!

> *Tip:* If you have any leftover pesto, seal it in an airtight container and pop it in the fridge for up to a few days in the freezer for a few weeks. Also, if you don't have walnuts for the pesto, cashews, almonds or pine nuts will work well in its place!

Four Simple Dressings

Dressings are essentially Botox for salads. Just inject a few flavorful ingredients to a salad and you've got yourself a whole new meal. These four dressings are what I turn to most, especially when a little something extra is needed on a salad. Feel free to use these dressings for any other salad you make at home. Experiment and enjoy the dressings!

Lemon-Honey Dijon

The Lemon-Honey Dijon dressing works beautifully on just about anything, especially when paired with peppery arugula and any kind of cooked grain. As seen in the Peppery Arugula Salad recipe on page 103.

SERVES 1 / V, GF

1 tbsp (15 g) whole-grain Dijon mustard

1 tbsp (15 ml) lemon juice

1 tsp honey, or maple syrup is vegan

3 tbsp (45 ml) olive oil

Splash of water

Pinch of sea salt

Mix all the ingredients together in a small bowl. If you have any leftover dressing, seal it up in an airtight container and store in the fridge for up to a few days.

Yogurt and Dill

Yogurt and Dill dressing works with salads that lean more on the salty side. The herbs help balance the flavors of ingredients such as salty olives and capers. As seen in the Greek-Inspired Kale Salad recipe on page 107.

SERVES 1 / V, GF

¼ cup (60 ml) Greek yogurt, or use plain coconut yogurt if vegan

1 tbsp (15 ml) lemon juice

1–2 tbsp (15–30 ml) olive oil

½ tsp clove garlic, grated

1 tsp fresh dill, roughly chopped

Pinch of sea salt

Mix all the ingredients together in a small bowl. If you have any leftover dressing, seal it up in an airtight container and store in the fridge for up to a few days.

Creamy Tahini

Creamy Tahini is a dressing that's easily whipped together with cupboard ingredients. If the salad is on the lighter side, I'll add this to bulk it up.

SERVES 1 / V, GF

2 tbsp (23 g) tahini

2 tbsp (30 ml) water

2 tbsp (30 ml) olive oil

1 clove garlic, grated

1 tbsp (15 ml) apple cider vinegar

1 tsp honey, or maple syrup if vegan (optional, but I really enjoy it)

Mix all the ingredients together in a small bowl. If you have any leftover dressing, seal it up in an airtight container and store in the fridge for up to a few days.

Simple Lemon

The Simple Lemon dressing is just that. If a salad is already packed with flavor, this is a lovely addition—mellow enough that it never overwhelms the salad.

SERVES 1 / V, GF

Juice of 1 lemon

3 tbsp (45 ml) olive oil

Pinch of sea salt

Mix all the ingredients together in a small bowl. If you have any leftover dressing, seal it up in an airtight container and store in the fridge for up to a few days.

6

A Few Quickies for the Road

On-the-go energizing snacks and smoothies.

"Hangry" is a real condition. We've all been there. Although snapping at your family in the middle of a packed plaza in a foreign country makes for an entertaining story, the sheer look of terror on the faces of nearby pedestrians only helps to confirm the "Americans are crazy" theory. To prevent a sudden explosion of hangry behavior, I carry around these goodies for me and for anyone else who may be in need of a food break. All it takes is a bit of organization. Choose a night during the week to set aside an hour to make a few of these treats. If you're a fan of energy balls, then give the Honey and Lime (page 121) a go for a zesty spin. The Cherry and Date Breakfast Bars with Dark Chocolate (page 122) is lovely for those who also want a touch of sweetness come midday. For a heartier choice, the Raw Pistachio-Ginger Bars (page 118) are nothing short of snacking euphoria. Either way, these treats or one of the delicious smoothies will get you through the week satisfied and hangry free.

Raw Pistachio-Ginger Bars

Raw treats never do it for me. Just the word "raw" alone turns me sideways and I slowly back away from whoever just said the word. However, I will make an exception—hell, I'll even embrace raw treats—when they're heavily doused in spicy ginger, blended with dates (I'm already a fanatic for them) and have some nuts inside. Better yet, I haven't met a friend or family member who doesn't freak out when they take a bite of these raw ginger bars. They check all the boxes.

MAKES 8–10 BARS / V, GF

For the base

1 cup (150 g) Medjool dates, pitted

½ cup (75 g) cashews

½ cup (75 g) pistachios

1 tbsp (7 g) raw cacao powder

Sea salt

For the ginger layer

3½ tbsp (52 ml) coconut oil

3 tbsp (35 ml) honey, or maple syrup if vegan

2 tbsp (23 g) ginger powder

Pinch of sea salt

Handful of roasted pistachios, for topping (optional)

In a food processor, add all the ingredients for the base and blend until a large, sticky ball forms (about 30 seconds). Add the date mixture into a small lined baking pan and smooth it out until it forms one solid layer. Pop this into the freezer to set while you make the topping.

In a small saucepan over low heat, melt the coconut oil. Turn off the heat once the oil has melted and set this aside to cool for about 10 minutes. After 10 minutes, add in the honey, ginger and salt. Whisk until the batter becomes thick and well combined.

Take the nut base out of the freezer, pour the melted ginger on top and sprinkle with the roasted pistachios. Place this back in the freezer to set for 30 minutes. After it has set, cut into small bars. Store the bars in the freezer for up to a few weeks.

Also, if you're into chocolate, you can always drizzle a bit of melted chocolate on top of the bars for a decadent treat. I've done this and it's delicious!

Energy Balls, Two Ways

Energy balls are the gateway and hallmark of healthy eating. They're so trendy it isn't even funny. Everywhere you look: energy balls. Your local corner store: energy balls. Your neighbor's freezer: energy balls. Women's purses: energy balls. My purse: energy balls. They're ubiquitous, and for good reason. Just choose a nut or seed, blend with dates (binding the ingredients) and add in any flavor that calls out to you. Five minutes later you have a pretty great snack.

I've created two recipes for you here—one with citrus and spice, and the other a classic using cacao and almonds. From this, adapt the recipes as you wish. Maybe add some orange zest or coconut shreds to your next batch. You really can't go wrong.

MAKES 12 BALLS / V, GF

Honey and Lime Energy Balls

1 cup (150 g) cashews

1 cup (150 g) Medjool dates, pitted

1 tsp ginger root, grated

1 tsp honey, or maple syrup if vegan

Zest of 1 lime and juice of ½ that lime

Pinch of sea salt

Classic Hazelnut and Cacao Energy Balls

1⅓ cups (200 g) Medjool dates, pitted

½ cup (75 g) almonds

½ cup (75 g) hazelnuts

2 tbsp (14 g) raw cacao powder

1½ tbsp (23 ml) water

1 tsp cinnamon powder

Pinch of sea salt

To prepare the energy balls for both recipes, simply add all the ingredients into the food processor and blend for about 15 to 20 seconds. We want the nuts to break down, but not turn into a creamy texture. There should be small pieces of nuts, adding texture to the balls. Roll into medium-sized balls and pop them into the refrigerator to set for at least an hour, or ideally overnight. Store in the fridge or freezer for up to a few weeks. I love these guys as a pre-workout snack, or really for any time of the day.

Cherry and Date Breakfast Bars with Dark Chocolate

If you're going over to a friend's home for dinner and you need to bring something, bring these bars. Or if you just want to make a friend a *best* friend, bring these bars.

I know that these bars are intended for breakfast, but over the past few months I've been packing them up and bringing them everywhere. Not just for breakfast, but also as a healthy snack on long drives, as an after-dinner treat and yes, I absolutely bring them every time I visit a friend. I know now that because of these bars, my friendships are stronger than ever … I joke. But in all honestly, try it for yourself and you'll know what I'm talking about.

MAKES 10–12 BARS / V, GF

1½ cups (225 g) Medjool dates, pitted

½ cup (130 g) cashew butter (or any nut butter, it will just change the overall flavor)

2 tbsp (30 ml) coconut oil, melted

Handful of pecans, chopped (optional)

1 cup (22 g) puffed brown rice or puffed quinoa

1 cup (150 g) dried cherries

Sea salt

3 oz (85 g) bar of dark chocolate, roughly chopped

¼ cup (60 ml) water

In the food processor, blend the dates, cashew butter and melted coconut oil until well combined, about 30 seconds. Now add the pecans, puffed rice and cherries into the food processor and pulse 5 to 6 times, just enough so that everything is well incorporated.

Pour the mixture into a medium-sized baking pan lined with parchment paper, and smooth it out until it forms one solid layer (should be about ½ inch [13 mm] thick). Pop this into the freezer to set for 15 minutes.

In the meantime, melt the chocolate using the double boiler method. Fill a small saucepan with ¼ cup (60 ml) of water and place a separate glass or metal bowl on top, covering the saucepan below. Once the top bowl is hot and the water below is boiling, add the chocolate to the bowl and let it melt, stirring slowly. Remove the chocolate sauce from the heat right after it has melted. Pour it evenly over the date and cherry layer. Pop this back in the freezer to set for another 15 minutes. Once it has set, cut into small bars. Enjoy on your way to work, school or wherever you're headed!

Tip: Use vegan dark chocolate to make these bars completely vegan.

Blueberry and Cacao Smoothie

The story of my birth goes something like this ... my mom goes into labor, my dad rushes her to the hospital, but on the way over my mom, being the chocolate fiend that she is, insists they stop at the nearest See's Candies for chocolate. FOR CHOCOLATE. So I entered this world, quite literally, as a screaming sugar monster. And nothing has changed since. I kid.

Naturally, I'd find a way to add chocolate into a smoothie. And why not? Strawberries taste good with chocolate, so do avocados apparently, and along this line of thinking blueberries *must* taste good with chocolate. As it turns out, they really do. Along with the blueberries, swirl into the smoothie a little almond butter and coconut yogurt. Now you have yourself a near-chocolate milkshake, with a side of fruit.

SERVES 1 / V, GF

1 cup (150 g) frozen blueberries

1 frozen banana, chopped

¾ cup (180 ml) almond milk

1 heaping tbsp (12 g) almond butter or any nut butter

1 tbsp (7 g) raw cacao powder

1 heaping tbsp (15 ml) yogurt of your choice

2 Medjool dates, pitted

Place all the ingredients into a blender and blend on high speed until it is completely smooth and there are no banana clumps.

Pour into a glass or bowl, and top with whatever you'd like! I love adding coconut shreds, cacao nibs and blueberries.

Tip: Use coconut yogurt to make this smoothie completely vegan.

La Dolce Vita Drink: Sweet Almond, Cinnamon and Yogurt Drink

When I was nineteen, I devised a plan to open a smoothie company that would sell to every Whole Foods in America. It was going to be big. Instead I left to study abroad and totally forgot about my youthful dreams. That is, until I stumbled upon a tiny shop in Italy that sold smoothies! And I don't mean a gelato shop that also offered smoothies, but a stand-alone smoothie cafe.

From the cobblestone streets of a very ancient city, where the newest addition was a built-in ATM machine, the sight of an L.A.-style smoothie shop was quite humorous. Nonetheless, I went in and ordered a smoothie. Aside from fresh pasta, it was the best thing I had in Italy all year. Sweet almonds blend together with bananas, cinnamon and honey, creating a surprisingly sinful drink. It's very luscious and will probably be the best thing you'll taste all day long.

SERVES 1 / V, GF

1 small banana

¾ cup (180 ml) almond milk

Small handful of almonds

1 tsp honey, or maple syrup if vegan

1 tsp cinnamon

1 heaping scoop of yogurt of your choice

A few ice cubes

Place all the ingredients into a blender and blend on high speed until it is nearly smooth with just a few almond pieces still intact. Pour into a glass and enjoy immediately!

Tip: Add a few scoops of plant-based protein powder for an extra boost in the morning! I opt for vanilla-flavor protein powder for this smoothie.

Raspberry-Basil Smoothie

Want one sure way to make smoothies captivating? Add some herbs, like basil. Basil is a great counterpart to a fruit-filled smoothie. It lends an earthiness that is peppery, yet sweet. Not overwhelming, but subtle enough that if you pass it over to a friend for a taste, they'll wonder what exactly you've snuck into it. It is a delightful departure from an everyday fruit smoothie blend. And if you are having trouble finding fresh basil, try some mint leaves, which taste just as great.

SERVES 1 / V, GF

1 cup (150 g) frozen raspberries

1 frozen banana, chopped

¾ cup (180 ml) almond milk

Small handful of fresh basil leaves

Place all the ingredients into a blender and blend on high speed until it is completely smooth and there are no banana or basil pieces. Pour into a glass and enjoy immediately!

Tip: If you can't find raspberries, feel free to swap them for strawberries.

7

Dessert

Enough said.

Dessert runs deep for me. It's not always a particularly flattering engagement. As a testament to my long-standing sweets affair, my own grandma banned me from indulging in her See's Candies holiday boxes. I've been known to poke holes underneath each truffle to see if it is the flavor I want, and if not, I leave it for an unsuspecting family member to eat. I don't blame her.

So you see, this chapter has been long anticipated—partly to sate my own desires and, hopefully, to satisfy yours. Whether you're a chocolate fanatic (right there with you) or your sweets profile veers more to the fruity side, I have something special for you. Each dessert is created to celebrate natural foods. Not one bit of refined sugar or flour here. If you're a chocolate purist, then Homemade Dark Chocolate with Lime Zest and Pumpkin Seeds (page 148) is an excellent choice to start with. Perhaps you'd like a lighter dessert; then the Peach-Cardamom Galette (page 135) is lovely. Or maybe meet in the middle with the Date-Glazed Chocolate Doughnuts with Cinnamon-Spiced Crushed Nuts (page 132). With nuts on top it could almost double as breakfast ... almost.

Date-Glazed Chocolate Doughnuts with Cinnamon-Spiced Crushed Nuts

From kindergarten to fifth grade, my breakfast consisted of Twinkies, Ding-Dongs, Hostess cupcakes or maple-glazed doughnuts. Unbeknownst to my mom, on the drive to school my dad would pull over to the corner store and pick up one of these treats, solidifying his role as *the best dad ever*. In seconds, the sugar-laden goods were taken down in a blaze of glory, and my sister and I emerged for air with "breakfast" all over our faces and doughnut wrappers littering the car floor. It was glorious.

Now as a woman in my 20s, I realize that starting each day with a Twinkie would probably frighten most adult humans. So let's call this recipe a happy compromise. These doughnuts are baked, adorned with healthy nuts and made with dates for a delicious glaze—a far cry from the classic treats of my youth.

MAKES 12 / V

For the date glaze
2 cups (300 g) Medjool dates, pitted
¾ cup (180 ml) boiling water
1 tbsp (12 g) cashew nut butter or tahini

For the chocolate doughnut
1 cup (250 ml) almond milk
1¼ cups (150 g) spelt flour
1 egg, or 1 flax egg if vegan (page 188)
¼ cup (60 ml) coconut oil, melted, plus more for greasing
½ cup (55 g) raw cacao powder
2 tsp (7 g) baking powder
½ tsp baking soda
1 tsp apple cider vinegar
⅓ cup (65 g) coconut sugar
Pinch of cinnamon powder
Pinch of sea salt

For the crushed nuts
2 cups (240 g) mixed nuts (I like a mix of pecans, walnuts and pistachios), chopped
4 tbsp (60 ml) maple syrup
2 tsp (5 g) cinnamon powder
Sea salt

Start by preheating the oven to 350°F (177°C). To make the glaze, mix the dates with the boiling water and leave to soak for 10 minutes. Then put them into a blender or food processor with the nut butter and blend until smooth and creamy.

Set this aside while you make the doughnut batter. Simply mix all the ingredients together in a medium-sized mixing bowl. Now grease the doughnut pans with the extra coconut oil. Fill the donut pan holes with the batter and pop into the oven to cook for 13 to 15 minutes.

Once they're done cooking, set aside while you roast the nuts. On a lined baking sheet, mix the nuts with the maple, cinnamon and salt, and cook at 350°F (177°C) for 8 to 10 minutes, or until golden brown but not burnt. Remove from the oven and let cool for about 10 minutes.

Now frost the doughnuts with the date glaze and top with the crushed nuts. Store the remaining doughnuts in an airtight container on your counter until you're ready for more!

Peach-Cardamom Galette

I'm still shocked whenever someone confesses that they, in fact, do not like chocolate. It's as if they're speaking Martian and I *really* cannot relate. Yet, these are the best people to dine with because, come dessert, you know they aren't going to stick their forks in your chocolate cake. Dining satisfaction—dessert for one!

This peach and cardamom galette is for those who would rather indulge in decadent stewed fruit. The sweet aroma of caramelized peaches and spicy cardamom are captured beneath a flaky, golden crust.

SERVES 4–6 SLICES / V

For the crust

1¼ cups (150 g) spelt flour

1½ tbsp (15 g) coconut sugar

Zest of 1 lemon

½ tsp cinnamon

Dash of cardamom

¼ cup (60 ml) coconut oil

6 tbsp (90 ml) ice water

Pinch of sea salt

For the filling

1 large peach, or nectarine, cut into thin slices

1 tbsp (8 g) spelt flour

2 tbsp (30 ml) maple syrup

1 tsp cinnamon powder

¼ tsp cardamom powder

½ tsp vanilla powder or vanilla extract

Dash of clove powder

1 tbsp (15 ml) coconut oil, divided in 4 (for the topping)

Coconut sugar, for dusting on crust

Start by preparing the dough for the crust and preheat the oven to 350°F (177°C). Mix all the dry ingredients for the crust into a large bowl. Melt the coconut oil and let it cool. Once it has cooled, pour the oil into the mixing bowl in fourths. With each pour of oil, mix the flour evenly between your fingers, creating smaller pieces of crumbly dough—pouring and mixing with your fingers a total of 4 times. Then slowly add the ice water—using the same mixing method with your fingers. Be careful not to overmix the dough. Form a ball and let it sit in the refrigerator for 20 minutes. Do not let it sit longer than 30 minutes, or else the dough becomes very hard to roll out.

Remove the dough from the refrigerator and roll into a flat circle (about 12 inches wide [30 cm] and ¼ inch [6 mm] thick) on a cutting board dusted with spelt flour.

Now mix all the filling ingredients (except the coconut oil) into a bowl with the sliced peaches. Place the peach slices in the center of the dough, forming a circle. Then gently fold the edges of the crust over the outer edges of the peaches (as seen in the photo). Add the remaining coconut oil on top of the peaches in four different spots. Sprinkle the crust with coconut sugar and then bake for 20 minutes until the fruit has stewed down and the crust is golden and flaky. Cut the galette into slices and enjoy!

Pralines and Cream with Chocolate "Magic" Shell

You know those foods that just don't do it for you? Well for me, it's ice cream and Mexican food. I absolutely never crave either, but whenever someone puts a bowl of pralines and cream or a bean burrito with guacamole in my face, I just stop and laugh at myself because both are excellent. With this dessert, I am rectifying my aversion towards ice cream by amplifying its deliciousness with a shell of chocolate sauce. When you melt down coconut oil, cacao powder and maple syrup and then pour it over ice cream, it hardens into a beautiful chocolate shell resembling a glorious and edible third-grade science experiment.

SERVES 6–7 / V, GF

For the Pralines and Cream

2 (14-oz [400-g]) cans full-fat coconut milk, chilled overnight in the fridge

½ cup (90 g) cashew nut butter or tahini

½ cup (120 ml) maple syrup

2 tbsp (30 ml) coconut oil, melted

1 tsp vanilla powder or vanilla extract

Pinch of sea salt

½ cup (75 g) Medjool dates, pitted

Handful of pecans

For the magic shell (serves 2)

2 tbsp (30 ml) coconut oil

3 tbsp (20 g) raw cacao powder

1½ tbsp (23 ml) maple syrup

Pinch of sea salt

Remove the chilled coconut milk from the fridge and scoop out the solid cream layer from the can. We want to use only the cream and discard the water (or save for a smoothie).

Place all the ingredients in a blender, except the dates and pecans, and blend for about 30 seconds, making sure everything is very well combined. Then toss in the dates and blend for 10 seconds, breaking down the dates into chunks. Toss in the pecans and blend for 5 seconds, breaking the nuts into pieces as well.

Now pour the ice cream mixture into a freezer-safe bowl and freeze for at least 3 hours, mixing the ice cream every 30 minutes. This helps the ice cream remain creamy and not overly icy.

Once you're ready to eat your ice cream, make the magic shell. In a small saucepan over low heat, melt the coconut oil and then remove it from the heat and stir in the remaining ingredients. Pour the chocolate sauce into a small cup and let it cool in the fridge for 10 minutes.

Now scoop the ice cream into cups and gently pour the cooled chocolate sauce on top and watch it slowly harden. It takes about 30 seconds. Magic!

Tip: If you don't have all the ingredients for the magic shell, you can always make it by melting 100 grams of dark chocolate with 1 tablespoon (15 ml) of coconut oil over low heat. Then pour! Also make sure that your coconut milk is chilled before making the recipe, otherwise the ice cream won't freeze completely. Although this is a healthy version of ice cream, there is still quite a bit of healthy fat, so I would suggest having a small helping and savoring the flavor.

Pralines and Cream Affogato

Affogato is the Italian word for "drowned." The only way to make drowning sound appealing is by submerging a cup of ice cream with a steamy shot of espresso. An effortless dessert of slowly melted ice cream enveloped in warm espresso—need I say more?

SERVES 2 / V, GF

2 scoops of the Pralines and Cream (page 136)

2 shots of hot espresso or ½ cup (120 ml) very strongly brewed coffee

Simply scoop the ice cream into a bowl and pour the hot espresso on top. Watch as it melts and turns into a luscious cream. I also like to add a sprinkling of nuts on top or even a few shavings of dark chocolate. Have at it!

Blackberry-Coconut Crisp

For anyone with a sweet tooth, I'm sure you can appreciate a dessert that nearly doubles as breakfast, which seems like a resourceful way to live. Fresh blackberries and blueberries bubble below a layer of toasted coconut and oats—this most certainly could be a breakfast or a healthy dessert—you choose. Either way you see it, stewed berries with a crispy topping is an undeniably delicious treat.

SERVES 6 / V, GF

For the topping

¾ cup (57 g) unsweetened coconut shreds

1½ cups (120 g) rolled oats

¼ cup (60 ml) maple syrup

¼ cup (60 ml) coconut oil, melted

1 tbsp (15 ml) vanilla powder, or extract

1 tsp cinnamon powder

Pinch of sea salt

For the filling

3 cups (450 g) blackberries

3 cups (450 g) blueberries

⅓ cup (80 ml) maple syrup

Juice of ½ lemon

1 tbsp (15 ml) vanilla powder, or extract

Pinch of sea salt

Preheat your oven to 350°F (177°C). Start making the topping by adding all the ingredients into a mixing bowl and combine.

For the filling, gently mix all the ingredients together in a bowl. Now pour the filling into a saucepan with 1 tablespoon (15 ml) of water. Keep the heat on high until the berries start to bubble, then lower to medium heat and cook for about 5 minutes, or until the berries start to release their juices and bubble. Stir occasionally.

Now pour the filling into a medium-sized baking dish and top with the coconut topping. Bake in the oven for 30 to 35 minutes, or until the top is slightly golden-brown. Let this cool for about 10 minutes and then serve with anything you'd like! Maybe go for the Pralines and Cream (page 136)!

Pralines and Cream over Sticky Date Cake

I've realized that this cake is something you're going to want to have down in your dessert repertoire. Dessert novice or not, a straightforward cake recipe is always appreciated. Take some dates along with a few other ingredients, mix together well and bake for nearly an hour. The dates caramelize into flavorful pockets with notes of toffee. Finish it off with a scoop of pralines and cream and call it a night.

SERVES 6–8 / V

1¼ cups (190 g) Medjool dates, pitted

1 cup (240 ml) water

1 tsp baking soda

1 tsp baking powder

1 egg, or flax egg if vegan (page 188)

½ tsp vanilla powder, or vanilla extract

¾ cup (150 g) coconut sugar

1 cup (120 g) spelt flour

Pinch of sea salt

Pralines and Cream (page 136), for topping

Start by preheating your oven to 350°F (177°C). In a food processor or blender, add in the dates, water, baking soda and powder, and mix until well combined, about 30 seconds.

In a separate bowl, mix together the egg, vanilla and sugar. Using a hand mixer on the highest speed, whisk the three ingredients together for a minute, until it becomes fluffy and paler in color. Then stir in the flour, the date mixture and salt to this bowl.

Pour the batter into a small baking dish (11 x 11 inch [28 x 28 cm]) that has been greased with coconut oil (so that batter doesn't stick when cooked). Bake for about 30 to 35 minutes, or until the center of the cake is moist. If you're using a different size pan, the temperature may vary. Keep an eye on the cake to see if it has cooked through. Take a knife and stick it into the center of the cake; if it comes out clean it is fully cooked.

Remove from the oven and let cool for at least 10 minutes. Top with the Pralines and Cream!

Coco-Macadamia-Nut "Ranger" Cookies

I feel that it is necessary in life to know how to make a really good cookie. A good cookie remedies almost anything. Remember when you got dumped and your best friend brought over baked cookies or at least an uncooked cookie dough log? I bet you felt a little better. Or when you failed a test and then headed right on over to the cupboard for a cookie? Good choice. Or hey, maybe you even rear-ended a car? Well maybe if you had a cookie on you to give to the person you rear-ended, the accident wouldn't have been *that* bad.

Overall, cookies are a good choice. And this Ranger cookie is loaded with the works. A mix of oats and coconut gives the cookie a hearty texture, while the macadamia nuts and puffed quinoa provide a crunch. And why not add in chocolate chips, keeping it within the classic cookie category. It might be an exaggeration to say that your life will be better with these cookies in it, but all I know for certain is that it definitely doesn't hurt.

Makes 14 Cookies / V, GF

¾ cup (90 g) almond flour

½ cup (60 g) oat flour

½ tsp baking powder

½ tsp baking soda

½ cup (40 g) rolled oats

¾ cup (57 g) unsweetened desiccated coconut shreds

1 egg, or flax egg if vegan (page xx)

1 tsp vanilla powder, or vanilla extract

½ cup (100 g) coconut sugar

½ cup (120 ml) coconut oil, melted

½ cup (10 g) puffed quinoa or puffed brown rice

⅓ cup (40 g) macadamia nuts, chopped

2 handfuls of dark chocolate pieces

Sea salt

Preheat the oven to 375°F (190°C) and line a baking sheet with parchment paper. In a medium-sized mixing bowl, toss together the almond flour, oat flour, baking soda and powder, rolled oats and coconut. Mix well.

In a separate bowl, cream together the egg, vanilla and sugar. Using a hand mixer on the highest speed, whisk the three ingredients together for a minute, until it becomes a bit fluffy and paler in color. Now mix in the melted coconut oil. Add the wet ingredients to the dry ingredients and mix. Stir in the puffed quinoa, macadamia nuts, chocolate pieces and a sprinkling of sea salt.

On a lined baking sheet, roll about 3 to 4 tablespoons (22 to 30 g) of dough between your hands into large-sized balls. Place on the lined baking sheet with about 2 inches (5 cm) of space between each cookie. Bake for 8 to 10 minutes. Remove from the oven and let cool. Enjoy with a glass of Macadamia-Almond Nut Milk (page 46).

Peanut Butter–Chocolate Fudge Slices

Show me a jar of peanut butter and I will show you how to use the entire thing in 15 minutes. To put this recipe into perspective, it makes *a lot* of fudge. And when I say fudge, it's more like whipped peanut butter mixed with puffed brown rice, then smothered in a layer of chocolaty peanut butter sauce and, last, sprinkled with peanuts. So if you don't like peanuts, this is probably *not* the recipe for you. But if you do like peanuts, then you most definitely hit the jackpot.

MAKES 10–12 SLICES / V, GF

For the peanut butter layer

1¼ cups (225 g) peanut butter

1 cup (100 g) almond flour

4 tbsp (60 ml) coconut oil

4 tbsp (60 ml) maple syrup

3 tbsp (45 ml) water

4 tbsp (28 g) raw cacao powder

5 Medjool dates, pitted

2 cups (40 g) puffed brown rice

2 small handfuls of peanuts, plus 1 handful saved for topping

Pinch of sea salt

For the chocolate fudge layer

6 tbsp (90 ml) coconut oil

½ cup (55 g) raw cacao powder

6 tbsp (90 ml) maple syrup

3–4 tbsp (33–45 g) peanut butter

Sea salt

To make the peanut butter layer, add to the food processor the peanut butter, almond flour, coconut oil, maple syrup, water, cacao and dates. Blend until creamy, about 20 seconds. Then add in the puffed brown rice, two handfuls of peanuts and sea salt. Pulse for about 5 to 10 seconds. We do not want to break down the rice or peanuts completely—we just want to mix them into the fudge.

Remove the peanut butter fudge from the food processor and scoop it onto a small lined baking pan. Smooth out the fudge until it forms one solid layer, about ¾ inch (19 mm) thick. Pop this into the freezer to set while you make the topping.

In the meantime, make the chocolate fudge layer. In a small saucepan over low heat, melt the coconut oil. Turn off the heat once the oil has melted and whisk in the rest of the ingredients for the chocolate fudge. Mix until the fudge becomes thick and well combined.

Take the peanut butter base out of the freezer and pour the chocolate fudge on top. Top with the extra peanut pieces and place this back in the freezer to set for 20 minutes. After it has set, cut into small chunks. Leave the slices in the freezer for up to a few weeks.

Tip: You can substitute any other nuts for the peanuts for any nut, making this a multi-nut butter fudge.

Homemade Dark Chocolate with Lime Zest and Pumpkin Seeds

Remember your first grown up job? Remember accepting it while thinking that you're on your way to raking in the big bucks, living in a penthouse apartment with a butler and a French bulldog … Well I ended up selling chocolate. Suffice it to say that reality set in *really* fast and my dreams of living it big, bumping shoulders with Beyoncé at the clubs in Paris over the weekends, faded as soon as my first check arrived.

Good thing I had an endless supply of chocolate-lime bars to comfort me through my reality check. Never before had I thought to add lime to chocolate. Just a touch goes a long way, brightening up a fresh batch of chocolate. Now nothing reminds me of the inflated dreams of life in my early 20s more than zesty chocolate-lime bars.

MAKES 10–12 / V, GF

1 cup (180 g) cacao butter

1¼ cups (140 g) cacao powder

Zest of 1 lime and juice of half that lime

¾ cup (180 ml) maple syrup

Pinch of sea salt

2 handfuls of raw pumpkin seeds

1 handful of pistachios

½ cup (10 g) puffed quinoa (optional but so good!)

Start by melting the cacao butter in a small saucepan over medium-low heat. Once it has melted, remove it from the heat and stir in the cacao powder, lime zest, juice, maple syrup and salt for 1 minute, or until the chocolate thickens.

Then mix in most of the pumpkin seeds, pistachios and puffed quinoa, saving a few to sprinkle on top. Line a medium-sized baking sheet with parchment paper. Pour the mix onto the baking sheet and top with the remaining pumpkin seeds, pistachios and puffed quinoa. The chocolate should be about ¾-inch (19-mm) thick. Leave this to set in the freezer for an hour. Once it has set, cut into small bars!

Tip: Although these chocolates will not melt (thanks to the cacao butter), I like keeping them in the refrigerator to nibble on throughout the day, keeping them fresh and a little crisp.

Midnight Chocolate Mousse Pots with Sweet Tahini Cream

I've completely abandoned the birthday cake tradition and swapped it for these mini chocolate mousse pots. They're a decadent treat whipped up in no time. Prepare them the night before for a fuss-free dessert that's ready when you need it. The best part? The sweet tahini cream speckled with black sesame seeds. I make it just so I can have a scoop of that topping.

SERVES 2–3 / V, GF

For the chocolate mousse

8 oz (227 g) dark chocolate of choice, roughly chopped

1 cup (240 ml) almond milk

½ tsp cinnamon powder

For the sweet tahini cream

½ (14-oz [400-g]) can full-fat coconut milk, chilled overnight in the fridge

1 heaping tbsp (12 g) tahini

½ tsp vanilla powder, or vanilla extract

1 tbsp (15 ml) maple syrup

½ tsp black sesame seeds

Start making the chocolate mousse by using the double boiler method to melt the chocolate. Fill a small saucepan with ¼ cup (60 ml) of water and place a separate glass or metal bowl on top, covering the saucepan below. Once the top bowl is hot and the water below is boiling, add the chopped chocolate to the bowl and let it melt, stirring slowly. Remove the chocolate sauce from the heat right after it has melted, and stir in the almond milk and cinnamon. Mix well and pour this into a deep mixing bowl.

Using a hand mixer or a mixing stand, whip the chocolate for about 4 minutes on the highest speed until most of the bubbles in the chocolate have disappeared. Even if they don't all disappear after 4 minutes, it's okay to stop. Be sure to wear an apron and clothes that you don't care for, because this part is very messy! Since the chocolate always gets on me, most times I place a towel over my hands and the mixing bowl as I whisk the chocolate with the hand mixer so that it doesn't splash all over the house.

Once you're done mixing, pour the chocolate into cups. Set them in the fridge for at least 3 hours to set.

Once you're ready to serve the mousse, quickly prepare the whipped cream. Remove the chilled coconut milk from the fridge and scoop out the solid cream layer from the can. We only want to use the cream, so discard the water (or save for a smoothie). Add this cream, along with the rest of the ingredients, except for the sesame seeds, and blend with a hand mixer (or in a blender) until creamy, about 1 minute. Stir in the sesame seeds. Scoop the whipped cream on top of the chocolate pots and enjoy.

Tip: Use vegan chocolate to make this dessert completely vegan.

8

Egg-stasy
Just throw an egg on it.

Has there ever been a food that's suffered backlash from millions quite like the modest egg? I mean, the egg debate is endless and the controversy is similar to that around which Spice Girls member you like the most.

Yes I know, I am exaggerating, but all I can say for certain is that many meals would have suffered the fate of the trash can if it weren't for the humble, always there when you need it, egg. Just throw an egg on top of pretty much any food and, with minimal effort, your meal just became infinitely better. What do savory green-onion pancakes need? Eggs. What would taste great on freshly baked sourdough? Eggs. And what would shakshuka be without its quintessential egg? Just plain tomato stew.

So you see, eggs do have their place in the culinary world. If you're new to the egg scene, I'd try the Little Veggie Egg Muffins (page 154). They are delicious and make you see eggs in a new light—as portable breakfasts on the go, stuffed with veggies. But if you're a unicorn, one who never abandoned eggs at the height of each scandal, then I'd suggest the Curried Egg Salad with Fresh Mint over Toast (page 157) for a flavorful affair that is heavy on the eggs.

Shopping Tip: More often than not, I've found the most flavorful eggs come from vendors at local farmers' markets. If this isn't an option, I'd recommend purchasing eggs that are organic, free of antibiotics and are non-GMO.

Little Veggie Egg Muffins

What is it about grandmas and their endless generosity for satisfying your fast-food cravings? Back in the day, my cousins and I exploded with enthusiasm, as only eight-year-olds do, for a breakfast drive-through. And we all chose the egg muffins with hash browns and orange juice. A classic combo.

These little egg muffins are a riff on that breakfast and obviously are far better on the body, to put it nicely. No side of sausage or meat here—just a simple egg muffin as the perfect vehicle, showcasing the charm of a few veggies. And all you need are kitchen basics: eggs, a few greens, mushrooms and a muffin tin. These little egg muffins come together quickly and work as a portable breakfast for when you're pressed for time, so no fast-food drive-by is needed.

Makes 10 / VEG, GF

2 tbsp (30 ml) olive oil

1 fennel bulb, quartered and thinly sliced

½ cup (75 g) green beans, chopped into thirds

Chili flakes

½–1 tsp sea salt

1 cup (66 g) cremini mushrooms, thinly sliced and chopped into tiny pieces

Handful of spinach

8 eggs

10 muffin liners or coconut oil to coat the muffin pan

Preheat your oven to 350°F (175°C) and line the muffin pans. If you don't have muffin liners, then simply rub the sides of the muffin tins with coconut oil. Start by warming the olive oil over medium-high heat in a medium-sized sauté pan. Add in the fennel, green beans, chili flakes and sea salt, and cook for 5 minutes. Then add in the mushrooms and spinach, and sauté for another 5 minutes on medium heat. If the pan ever dries out, add a few splashes of water and mix well. Once the veggies have cooked down into tender pieces but still hold a slight crunch, set them aside to cool.

In a medium-sized bowl, whisk the eggs together with a fork for 1 minute. Stir in the veggies and slowly pour the batter into the lined muffin pans. Pour until the batter almost reaches the top.

Pop the pans into the oven to cook for 18 to 20 minutes, or until the tops are golden and the inside of the muffins are cooked through. Store in an airtight container in the fridge for when you want to enjoy them next!

Curried Egg Salad with Fresh Mint over Toast

I am so freaking proud of this recipe. I worked and reworked it so many times that I can't even tell you what the hell the original recipe consisted of. Maybe there was some dill in there? Definitely no crispy pears. And mint? Well, I have no idea how that made it into the recipe but it just works.

It's an egg salad that has just the right amount of flavors mingling about. Not too much curry—don't want to overwhelm the mint—and just enough crispy pear slices to cut through the soft egg. Have at it, but don't overgrate the eggs into a mushy mound, because nobody wants any bit of that.

SERVES 3–4 / VEG

4 hard-boiled eggs

2 green onion stalks, sliced into thin rings

½ crisp Asian pear, or crisp apple if not available

2–3 generous tbsp (5–7 g) fresh mint leaves, chopped, plus extra for topping

1 tbsp (12 g) curry powder

2½ tbsp (37 ml) Greek yogurt

Sea salt

3–4 sourdough slices, toasted

Using a cheese grater, grate the hard-boiled eggs into a bowl. Roughly chop the green onions, Asian pear and mint leaves into bite-size pieces, and add this to the bowl with the eggs. Mix in the curry powder, Greek yogurt and sea salt. Taste the egg salad and see if you'd like to add in more mint or sea salt depending on your taste buds. Serve on a thick slice of warm sourdough toast and top with a sprinkling of freshly chopped mint leaves.

Skillet Eggs with Garlicky Greens and Creamy Hummus

This is a true end-of-the-week meal for when you notice a few straggly greens in the back of the fridge that need to be cooked ASAP. Sautéed greens, mushrooms and tomatoes are the backbone of this dish, but we might as well crack an egg into the skillet for good measure. And since most weeks I have a big batch of leftover hummus, I like to finish this off with a layer of creamy hummus. Try this one out when you think all you can do with your dull greens is to toss them into the trash. Spices, an egg and maybe some hummus are all that's needed to bring them back to life.

SERVES 2 / VEG, GF

For the skillet eggs

2 tbsp (30 ml) olive oil

3 cloves garlic, roughly chopped

1 cup (150 g) cherry tomatoes, cut in half

Pinch of sea salt

3 large handfuls of kale leaves or Swiss chard, roughly chopped

1½ cups (115 g) mushrooms, thinly sliced

Sprinkling of red pepper flakes

Juice of ½ of a small lemon

2 eggs

For the creamy hummus

1 (14-oz [400-g]) can chickpeas

6 tbsp (67 g) tahini

6 tbsp (90 ml) olive oil

2 cloves garlic

2 tbsp water

Juice from ½ lemon

Sea salt

In a medium-large sauté pan on medium heat, warm the olive oil for 1 minute and add the garlic. Let this cook for about 1 minute. Then add the cherry tomatoes and a pinch of sea salt and sauté for about 5 minutes. If the bottom of the pan starts to dry out, simply add a splash of water and mix all the ingredients together.

Now add in the chopped kale, mushrooms, pepper flakes, lemon juice and a few splashes of water. Let this cook down for about 10 to 15 minutes. Once it's cooked, push the veggies to one side of the pan and crack the two eggs into the other side. Cook the eggs any style that you prefer—I like my eggs over easy.

In the meantime, make the creamy hummus. First rinse and drain the chickpeas and then combine all the ingredients in a food processor and blend until whipped and creamy, about 2 minutes. Taste the hummus to see if you'd like to add more salt, lemon juice or more water for a thinner hummus.

Dollop a small layer of hummus into a serving bowl and top with the skillet eggs and veggies.

Moroccan Spiced Shakshuka over Homemade Baba Ghanoush

I get a lot of mileage out of the Middle Eastern dish, shakshuka, especially as it only takes a few humble ingredients: canned tomatoes, eggs, onions and spices. Since the base of shakshuka is stewed tomatoes, add in any extra vegetables that you'd like. Zucchini, eggplant or even kale would be welcome additions. Here, I've included a creamy spread of homemade baba ghanoush to add richness to the dish.

SERVES 2–4 / VEG, GF

For the baba ghanoush

1 medium-sized eggplant

1 clove garlic

Juice of 1 lemon

2 tbsp (23 g) tahini

Handful of parsley leaves

2 tbsp (30 ml) olive oil

¼–½ tsp sea salt

For the shakshuka

2 tbsp (30 ml) olive oil

1 yellow onion, quartered and thinly sliced

1 tsp cumin powder

1 tsp coriander powder

1 tsp paprika powder

½ tsp cinnamon powder

½ tsp ginger powder

1 tbsp (15 ml) honey

1 tsp apple cider vinegar

Pinch of chili flakes

1 tbsp (15 g) tomato paste

Pinch of sea salt

1 (28-oz [800-g]) can chopped tomatoes

1½ cups (50 g) spinach

4 eggs

Zest of 1 lemon, for topping

Start by preparing the baba ghanoush. Preheat the oven to 450°F (232°C) and prick your eggplant several times with a fork (this prevents the eggplant from exploding in your oven). Place the whole eggplant on a baking pan and cook in the oven for 20 minutes.

For the shakshuka, warm the olive oil in a medium-sized saucepan on medium heat for 1 minute. Add the onions, all the spices, honey, apple cider vinegar, chili flakes, tomato paste and sea salt. Sauté for about 10 minutes, or until the onions are a bit translucent and have softened. If the bottom of the pan starts to dry out at any point, add a splash of water and mix all the ingredients together.

Add the canned tomatoes to the sauce pan and turn up the heat till it starts to boil. Now lower the heat to a simmer. Mix in the spinach and cook for another 15 minutes, or until the tomato sauce thickens. Taste the tomato sauce to see if you'd like to add more salt.

Now make 4 small holes in the tomato sauce and crack an egg into each hole. Cover the pan with a lid and let the eggs cook for about 5 minutes, or until the white part has cooked through and the yolk is firm but not fully cooked. Sprinkle the top of the shakshuka with the fresh lemon zest.

Now for the baba ghanoush. Once the eggplant has cooked, remove it from the oven and let it cool for a few minutes. Remove and discard the skin of the eggplant. Place the eggplant meat in a food processor along with the rest of the ingredients, and blend until whipped and creamy, about 30 seconds. Taste the baba ghanoush to see if you'd like to add a bit more salt or lemon juice.

Dollop a thin layer of the baba ghanoush into a serving bowl and top with the shakshuka.

Zesty Sweet Potato Hash with Caramelized Onions and Poached Egg

I might get some backlash from fellow San Franciscans for saying this, but SF is seriously lacking some healthy dinner eateries. Yeah, I know, we house some of the very best restaurants that focus on locally sourced ingredients. However, coating greens in vats of fat from the ankle of a pig on a nose-to-tail menu just somehow doesn't scream "healthy eating." More often than not, I'll heat up a sauté pan of caramelized onions while roasting cubes of sweet potatoes into a crispy-golden oblivion. Then grace the hash with a poached egg for a more balanced farm-to-table eating experience.

SERVES 2–3 / VEG, GF

4 tbsp (60 ml) ghee or olive oil, divided

2 large yellow onions, quartered and thinly sliced

Pinch of sea salt

2 large sweet potatoes

2 tsp (5 g) cumin

2 tsp (5 g) coriander

1 tsp paprika

Pinch of chili flakes

1 tbsp (15 ml) olive oil (for the sweet potatoes)

2–3 eggs

1 tsp vinegar (optional, for poached egg—I use white vinegar)

Juice of 1 lime

Handful of fresh cilantro

1 avocado, sliced

Start by making the caramelized onions. In a medium saucepan on medium heat, melt 2 tablespoons (30 ml) of ghee and add in the onion slices with a sprinkling of sea salt. Let the onions cook down for about 15 to 20 minutes. Stir the onions periodically. If the bottom of the pan dries out at any point, add a splash of water and mix all the ingredients together—this is where the caramel flavors lie.

In the meantime, preheat the oven to 425°F (218°C) and line a baking pan with parchment paper. Cut the sweet potatoes into small bite-size cubes and toss them into a mixing bowl, along with all the spices, olive oil and sea salt. Pour the spiced sweet potatoes on top of the baking pan and cook for about 30 to 40 minutes, or until the pieces are crispy and tender. Turn the batch halfway through.

Remove the sweet potatoes from the oven and mix them with the caramelized onions. Set this aside as you poach the eggs.

To perfectly poach your eggs, add the vinegar into a small pot of simmering water. Crack one egg into a ramekin or small cup. Using a spoon, create a whirlpool in the water—this will help the white part of the egg wrap around the yolk. Now slowly add the egg directly into the middle of the swirling water. Let it cook for 3 minutes. Remove the poached egg from the water and trim off any wispy white edges that didn't wrap around the yolk—this is needed only for the aesthetics of the dish.

In a serving bowl, place a generous helping of the sweet potato and onion hash, and add a poached egg. Top the meal off with a drizzle of lime juice, fresh cilantro and slices of avocado.

Savory Green Onion and Halloumi Pancakes with Poached Egg

The first time I experienced halloumi cheese, there was an older Greek man hunched behind a skillet, spatula flailing about in one hand and the other beckoning for me to come over to try the best of his Greek cuisine. I obliged. Hot from the sizzling pan arose a firm piece of white cheese that mimicked tofu in looks. He pierced it with a toothpick, handed it over and stared at me for approval. I gave it to him. That Greek man was right—halloumi cheese is *amazing*. My family is Italian, but given the choice, I'd trade balls of mozzarella for strips of halloumi. It's naturally salty, does not need extra seasoning and is so versatile in recipes. Enjoy it straight out of the skillet, on top of salads and lentils, or as you see here, mixed into green pancakes with a delicately poached egg on top.

MAKES 4–6 PANCAKES / VEG

3 cups (90 g) fresh spinach leaves

2 cups (220 g) halloumi cheese, grated

1 cup (50 g) green onions, roughly chopped

1 cup (120 g) spelt flour

1 egg

1 tbsp (12 g) baking powder

⅓–⅔ cup (80–160 ml) almond milk or water

4–6 tsp (20–30 ml) coconut oil or ghee, divided: 1 tbsp per pancake

4–6 eggs for poaching

1 tsp vinegar (optional, for poached egg—I use white vinegar)

Handful microgreens (optional)

Juice of 1 lime

Start wilting the spinach by warming it with a few splashes of water in a medium-sized sauté pan on medium-low heat. Once the spinach has wilted down, remove it from the pan and lay it between a few paper towels. Squeeze out as much water from the spinach as you can into the paper towels.

Into a mixing bowl, add the wilted spinach, cheese, green onions, spelt flour, egg, baking powder and almond milk. Mix until the ingredients are well combined.

In a medium-sized sauté pan on medium-high heat, melt the coconut oil. Add a few tablespoons of the batter and cook until the pancake is golden brown, about 3 to 4 minutes per side. Repeat this until all your batter is gone. Set your pancakes aside while you poach the eggs.

To perfectly poach your egg, add the vinegar into a small pot of simmering water. Crack one egg into a ramekin or small cup. Using a spoon, create a whirlpool in the water—this will help the white part of the egg wrap around the yolk. Now slowly add the egg directly into the middle of the swirling water. Let it cook for 3 minutes. Remove the poached egg from the water and trim off any wispy white edges that didn't wrap around the yolk—this is only for the aesthetics of the dish.

Serve the pancake with the poached egg on top, a sprinkling of microgreens and a squeeze of lime juice.

8

Fishing for a Compliment?
Seafood recipes that are simply off the hook.

My great-grandfather was a fisherman, and my father was a fishmonger. Me ... well, I still can't properly fillet a fish. Yet, I've never known a time in my life where seafood wasn't served as a side to any meal. Come November, fresh Dungeness crab made its way to the table with only a splash of red wine vinegar, olive oil and garlic. And every Christmas spent with my Italian-American family was a colossal celebration of the sea—cooking not one or two, but *seven* different fishes for the night.

Seafood marked a time for celebration. That's exactly how I still approach seafood today. I enjoy it as a side and celebrate it whenever it makes its way onto the table. When my friends pop in for a visit, I turn to the Shrimp and Chive Dumplings (page 180) for a last-minute taster, or the Cajun-Spiced Salmon Burrito with Garlic Prawns (page 175) for a heartier treat. Even my sister's husband, a skeptic of healthy cooking, took down that burrito as if it were loaded with Kobe beef.

This collection of seafood recipes is for you and anyone who'd like to tiptoe their way into the marine world of cooking. The recipes that ensue use a few herbs and spices to highlight the fish. Nothing too fancy is necessary. High-quality fish on its own brings vibrant flavors to the plate. Enjoy these recipes as a side to your veggies or as the high point to the meal.

Shopping Tip: When possible, try to source high-quality, wild-caught fish (salmon, shrimp, tuna, cod and halibut).

167

Mini Salmon Cakes Topped with Avocado Cream

There is only one way to put this … I freak out over this dish. I tried really hard not to play favorites but I feel compelled to confess that this is quite possibly my favorite recipe in the book. Not just within the seafood section, but the whole entire 200-page recipe book. It has e-v-e-r-y-t-h-i-n-g. Fish? Well, that's a given. Veggies? Yup. Fruit? Um-hm. Greens? Absolutely. It's a salad, it's a seafood side, it's honestly whatever you want it to be.

MAKES 8–10 CAKES / GF

For the salmon cakes

3 tbsp (45 ml) olive oil, divided

1 cup (150 g) celery, roughly diced

½ cup (75 g) red onion, diced

Pinch of sea salt

½ pound (230 g) cooked salmon (preferably wild-caught)

1 egg

2 tbsp (30 ml) whole-grain Dijon mustard

¼ cup (10 g) parsley, chopped

Pinch of chili flakes

For the avocado cream

2 avocados

Zest of ½ of a small lemon and the juice of this lemon

2 tbsp (30 ml) water

1 tbsp (15 ml) olive oil

Handful of fresh parsley

½ tsp sea salt

For the salad

3 cups (60 g) arugula

1 grapefruit

Drizzle of olive oil

Start by sautéing your veggies to prepare for the salmon cakes. In a medium-sized sauté pan over medium-high heat, warm 2 tablespoons (30 ml) of olive oil for 1 minute. Add the celery, onions and sea salt to the sauté pan. Cook for about 10 minutes, stirring occasionally. If the bottom of the pan dries out, add a splash of water.

In the meantime, in a large mixing bowl, flake the cooked salmon into small pieces. Add the sautéed celery mixture, egg, Dijon, parsley, chili flakes, 1 tablespoon (15 ml) of olive oil and a generous pinch of sea salt to the flaked salmon, and mix well. Form a ball with the salmon mixture and set this in the fridge for 30 minutes.

While the salmon sets, make the avocado cream. Simply add all the ingredients into a food processor and blend until creamy. Taste the cream and see if you'd like to add more salt, parsley, etc.

Remove the salmon mixture from the fridge and preheat the oven to 400°F (205°C) and line a baking sheet. To make the salmon cakes, simply roll about 3 to 4 tablespoons (45 to 60 g) of the mixture in your hands to form medium-sized cakes (as in the picture). Place each cake on the lined baking sheet and cook in the oven for about 10 to 12 minutes, or until the cakes are slightly golden-brown on top.

Now prepare the salad by adding the arugula to a large mixing bowl. Slice the grapefruit in half. Take one half of the grapefruit and remove its peel and then cut the meat of the grapefruit into bite-size pieces. Add to the salad. Make the dressing by squeezing the second half of the grapefruit over the salad and add a drizzle of olive oil.

I like to serve this dish individually. Place a bit of the salad on a small plate, top with 2 to 3 salmon cakes and top each salmon cake with a generous helping of the avocado cream. Enjoy this one!

Tip: Since these cakes are baked, they will be a bit more crumbly than fried salmon cakes. Be delicate when handling them after they are baked.

Halibut in Stewed Tomatoes, Capers and Olives over Spaghetti

Nothing takes me back to 2011, when I was living in Italy as a low-budget (a.k.a. broke), study-abroad student quite like this seafood pasta. This recipe became a staple and obsession of mine. Flaky halibut is lightly stewed in tomatoes and speckled with fresh basil and olives, showcasing the delicious simplicity of Italian cuisine. It's a recipe I know by heart and one that I make for friends who stop by for a quick dinner. They all become enamored with this dish. Forewarning, if you do make this for friends, double the recipe, because they will get a little feisty if there aren't leftovers to take home. *Buon appetito, amici.*

SERVES 2 / GF

3 tbsp (45 ml) olive oil

½ small red onion, quartered and thinly sliced

Pinch of sea salt

8 Roma-style tomatoes, or any medium-sized tomato

Pinch of chili flakes

½ pound (230 g) fresh or dry gluten-free spaghetti (optional)

1 tsp capers

6 Kalamata olives, roughly chopped

8 oz–10 oz (230–285 g) fresh halibut (1 medium-sized piece)

Handful of fresh basil leaves

In a medium-sized saucepan on medium-high heat, warm the olive oil with the onions and a pinch of sea salt for 5 minutes.

In the meantime, cut the top off each tomato and squeeze out all the juice and seeds from the inside and discard (I squeeze them out into the sink). Then roughly chop the tomatoes into large chunks and add them to the saucepan with a few tablespoons of water to keep the sauce moist. Turn up the heat to high. Once the tomato sauce starts to bubble, bring down the heat to a low simmer. Sprinkle with sea salt (about 1 teaspoon) and chili flakes and let this simmer for 15 minutes with the lid ajar. Every few minutes or so as the tomatoes cook down, press the tomatoes with the back end of a fork, smoothing out the tomato chunks and turning it into a sauce. If you can, remove and discard some of the tomato skins from the sauce as it cooks down. Add a few splashes of water to the sauce so that it doesn't stick to the pan.

Optional, if served with pasta: In the meantime, make the pasta. Add a tablespoon (15 g) of sea salt to a large pot of boiling water. Then toss in the spaghetti and cook for as long as the instructions require. Stir the pasta frequently as it cooks.

After the tomato sauce has cooked for 15 minutes, add in the capers, olives and halibut. Cook the halibut in the sauce, with the lid ajar, on low heat until it's tender, about 7 to 10 minutes depending on the size.

Once the fish is done cooking, flake the halibut into smaller pieces. Drain the pasta and top with the halibut sauce and basil leaves.

Tip: Adding the stewed fish to pasta is optional. Some days I'll make pasta if I want a heartier meal, but it also tastes delicious without.

Thai-Style Red Curry with Eggplant and Prawns

While I was writing this cookbook, on most Thursdays I would invite friends for a tasting. To sum it up, this Thai seafood curry surpassed all other recipes, even for the meat enthusiasts at the table, letting them relish a meal that usually calls for meat or chicken.

Perhaps its magic lies in that it's simply a curry recipe and everybody loves a good curry. Or maybe it's the cozy factor of warming up to a bowl of stewed seafood. Either way, a good curry has a way of pausing time from first bite to last, leaving you with a few moments of total food euphoria.

SERVES 4–6 / GF

2 tbsp (30 ml) coconut oil

2 shallots, or 1 small red onion, roughly chopped

Pinch of sea salt

3 cloves garlic, roughly chopped

1 knob of fresh ginger root, grated

½ red bell pepper

½ yellow bell pepper

2 medium-sized carrots

2 tbsp (30 g) red curry paste

2 tsp (8 g) coconut sugar

1 (14-oz [400-g]) can full-fat coconut milk

⅓ cup (80 ml) water

2 cups (60 g) green beans, cut in half with stems removed

1 cup (150 g) frozen peas

2 cups (150 g) spinach

½ pound (230 g) raw shrimp

Large handful of fresh cilantro, plus more for serving

Juice of ½ lemon

Brown rice or quinoa, for serving

In a large sauté pan (I like to use a Dutch oven) over medium-high heat, melt the coconut oil and add the shallots and a big pinch of sea salt. Mix around for a minute, then lower the heat to medium and add the garlic and ginger and cook for another minute.

Chop the bell peppers (discarding the tops and the seeds) into thin strips and then cut the strips in half. Cut the carrots into thin circles. Add both to the sauté pan along with the curry paste and sugar, and cook for a few minutes. Now bring the heat to high and add in the coconut milk, water, green beans and peas. Wait until the curry boils and then bring the heat down to a simmer. Let this cook for about 10 minutes, or until the green beans are tender.

Stir in the spinach, shrimp, cilantro and lemon juice. Cook until the shrimp are fully cooked through, about 3 minutes.

Serve over brown rice and top with fresh cilantro.

Tip: Red curry paste might be difficult to find at conventional markets, so first try to find it at any health food store or online.

Cajun-Spiced Salmon Burrito with Garlic Prawns and Chipotle Aioli

In London's Borough Market, there is a stall linked to a restaurant called Applebee's Fish (*not the American chain*) that serves hot wraps loaded with Cajun and garlic-spiced seafood—all for 7 dollars! This recipe is the closest thing I've made that mimics the deliciousness of that wrap. Although I have no idea when I'll return, I do know that I want this recipe in my life. Trust me, after you make this, you will, too.

SERVES 3–4 / GF

For the burrito

½ pound (230 g) raw salmon (preferably wild-caught)

½ tsp garlic powder

½ tsp paprika powder

¼ tsp cayenne powder

¼ tsp oregano powder

½ tsp coconut sugar

½ tsp red pepper flakes

Pinch of ground black pepper

4 tbsp (60 ml) olive oil, divided

Sea salt

⅓ head butter lettuce

1 tomato, sliced

3–4 burrito wraps of your choice (perhaps a gluten-free choice)

For the chipotle aioli

¾ cup (177 ml) Greek yogurt

1½ tsp (4 g) cumin powder

1–2 chipotle chili peppers in adobo sauce (2 if you like it very spicy)

Handful of fresh cilantro

Zest and juice of half a lemon

Pinch of sea salt

For the garlic prawns

2 tbsp (30 ml) olive oil

4 cloves garlic, roughly chopped

Sea salt

½ pound (230 g) raw shrimp

½ tsp garlic powder

Start by marinating your salmon. Rinse the salmon under water and pat dry. Cut the salmon into big chucks and toss them into a mixing bowl. Add in all the spices, 2 tablespoons (30 ml) of olive oil and mix well. Let this sit for a few minutes while you prepare the aioli.

Simply blend all the ingredients for the chipotle aioli in the food processor until creamy. Taste to see if you'd like to add any more lemon, salt, etc.

As the salmon marinates, cook the shrimp. In a medium-sized saucepan over medium heat, warm the olive oil for 1 minute. Add in the garlic, sea salt and shrimp. Bring the heat down to medium-low and cook the shrimp for about 2 to 3 minutes per side, until they've turned slightly pink in color. Add in the garlic powder after they have cooked and mix well. Once the shrimp have cooled, cut them into bite-size pieces.

Using the same sauté pan, warm the remaining olive oil for the salmon on medium-high heat. Bring the heat down to medium and toss the salmon chunks into the pan and cook until they turn pink in color, about 3 minutes on each side depending on the size.

To prepare the burrito, add a few pieces of butter lettuce and sliced tomatoes, a generous helping of the chipotle aioli and then as much salmon and shrimp as you'd like into the burrito wrap. Enjoy for breakfast, lunch or dinner!

Zesty Avocado and Orange Salad with Shrimp

This is a take on a popular recipe from my blog in which sautéed shrimp is mixed with chunks of papaya and scooped into an avocado. For this recipe, I've reached for accessible ingredients, making it more of a weekly meal option. Citrusy oranges are tossed with thin slices of fennel, adding a light crunch to the tender shrimp. Throw in some cubed avocado for a touch of creaminess and you have yourself a seafood salad that comes together in less than 15 minutes. Enjoy it as is or paired with the Honey-Roasted Carrots and Lentil Salad (page 61) for a heartier meal.

SERVES 4 / GF

For the shrimp

2 tbsp (30 ml) olive oil

1 small yellow onion, diced

1 pound (500 g) raw shrimp

Pinch of sea salt

For the salad

½ avocado, cubed

½ fennel bulb, quartered and thinly sliced

2 large oranges, divided

Drizzle of olive oil

Pinch of sea salt

In a medium-sized saucepan over medium-high heat, warm the olive oil for 1 minute. Add in the onions, shrimp and sea salt. Cook the shrimp for about 2 to 3 minutes per side, until they've turned slightly pink in color.

In a large mixing bowl, add in the avocado cubes and the fennel slices. Peel back the skin of the orange and cut the flesh of the orange into half pieces (discard the peel). Add in the orange slices from 1 orange to the bowl. Now cut the second orange in half and squeeze the juice from one half all over the salad. Add a drizzle of olive oil, a pinch of sea salt and mix well.

Add the shrimp to the salad—but not the onions. Mix the shrimp with the salad and serve immediately.

Tip: Since we don't add the sautéed onions to the salad, you can save and add them to an omelet or curry later in the week.

Crunchy Macadamia Halibut over Zesty Wild Rice and Snow Peas

I briefly dated a guy who lived on a boat, which made for an *interesting* experience. Bathroom situations were questionable and the kitchen situation was even more confusing. There's something about the amount of water a boat can store, coupled with rationing of shower use and gas, meaning that you use water sparingly. Wow, I am just as confused now just thinking about it as I was then. In short, I was a hot mess in that kitchen.

The only time I wasn't was when he made something similar to what you see here. Thank god I had that experience, because I love this fish dish, especially the zesty wild rice and caramelized fennel that accompany the halibut. No matter the size of your kitchen, boat-small or warehouse-big, you can make this fish, easy.

SERVES 4 / GF

For the rice with veggies

1 cup (200 g) wild rice

2 tbsp (30 ml) olive oil

½ fennel bulb, quartered and thinly sliced

½ red onion, quartered and thinly sliced

Pinch of sea salt

1½ cups (225 g) snow peas or sugar snap peas

2 cups (60 g) spinach leaves

¼ cup (60 ml) water

1 avocado, cubed

3 green onion stalks, chopped into rings

Zest of 1 lime and juice of ½ that lime, plus more for topping

Large handful of macadamia nuts, roughly chopped, plus more for topping

For the halibut

2 tbsp (30 ml) olive oil

2 cloves garlic, grated

1 knob of fresh ginger root, grated

Pinch of sea salt

2 medium-sized fillets of halibut (about ½ pound [230 g] total)

Start by cooking the wild rice by following the instructions on the box. Add ½ teaspoon of salt to the pot of water.

In the meantime, prepare the veggies for the rice. In a medium-sized sauté pan on medium-high heat, warm the olive oil for 1 minute. Add the fennel, onions and salt to the pan and sauté for 8 to 10 minutes, stirring occasionally. Now add the snow peas, spinach and about ¼ cup (60 ml) of water to the pan. Cook for another 5 to 8 minutes, or until the snow peas have softened but still hold a crunch. If the bottom of the pan begins to dry, add a splash of water.

Once the wild rice has cooked, add it to the sauté pan with the veggies. Stir in the avocado, green onions, lime zest, lime juice and macadamia nuts. Mix until everything is well combined. Taste the rice to see if you'd like to add more salt, lime juice, etc. Set this aside while you cook the fish.

Rinse the halibut pieces and pat them dry. In a small bowl, mix together the olive oil, garlic, ginger and a pinch of sea salt. Use a basting brush, or your fingers, and press the garlic-ginger paste all over the halibut. Make sure that it is well coated on both sides. In a medium-sized sauté pan over medium-high heat, cook the halibut for about 5 minutes per side, or until the halibut is cooked through and crispy on the outside.

Set the halibut on top of the wild rice and veggies, sprinkle with extra macadamia nuts and a drizzle of lime juice.

Shrimp and Chive Dumplings

For a few years, I spent every Sunday devouring plates of dumplings at a local dim sum spot. It became a ritual with one big problem. It was a spot I frequented with an ex. When that relationship ended, so did my Sunday dim sum. So I made a new ritual! Because what do you do when a relationship ends? You take the best part of it and make it even better.

Dumplings are not reserved for only Sundays now, but for any day of the week, because I got clever and learned how to make them. It's an extremely easy process. Mix together flavors you enjoy—in this case classic shrimp and chive—and twist them into little dumpling packets. If you don't have a steamer, I've listed alternative ways in the instructions to make them using a sauté pan.

MAKES 20–25 SMALL DUMPLINGS

2 cups (150 g) cabbage, grated

½ pound (250 g) raw shrimp

1 tsp sea salt

½ cup (25 g) chives, roughly chopped

½ cup (15 g) cilantro, roughly chopped

¼ cup (12 g) green onions, roughly chopped

1 tsp fresh ginger root, grated

2 cloves garlic, grated

1 tsp sesame oil or olive oil

Pinch of chili flakes

20–30 wonton or pot sticker wrappers

½ cup (120 ml) water, if using the sauté pan method

3 tbsp (45 ml) tamari (gluten-free soy sauce)

1 tsp sesame seeds (optional, for topping)

Start by boiling your cabbage to soften the leaves. Bring a medium-sized pot filled with water to a boil and toss in the cabbage. Cook for about 30 seconds. Remove the cabbage and press the leaves between two paper towels, squeezing out all the liquid you can. Repeat this process until most of the liquid had been removed from the cabbage leaves.

In the meantime, prepare your steamer for the dumplings. If you don't have a steamer, no worries, I have a sauté pan method for you.

To make the filling, add the shrimp, cooked cabbage, 1 teaspoon of sea salt and the rest of the ingredients (except the wontons, tamari and sesame seeds) into the food processor and pulse for about 10 seconds, incorporating all the ingredients.

For this recipe, I used circular wonton wrappers, but any wrappers will work. Depending on the size of your wonton wrapper, stuff the wontons with 1 to 2 teaspoons of filling. Dollop a small amount of the filling directly into the center of the wonton and lightly wet the wonton rim with water. Leave enough room around the wonton rim to be able to lift each side, pinching at the top. This is how you seal the wonton, creating a stuffed circular packet that is pinched at the top.

Now place your dumplings into the steamer basket and cook for about 2 to 3 minutes—just until the shrimp is cooked through.

If you don't have a steamer on hand, you can steam the dumplings in a medium-sized sauté pan. Bring the heat to high, pour in ½ cup (120 ml) of water and then add the dumplings. Cover the pan with a lid and cook for 3 minutes, or until most of the water has evaporated.

Remove the dumplings and serve them on a plate alongside the dipping sauce. In a small bowl simply mix together the tamari and sesame seeds, making the dipping sauce. Enjoy!

Tuna Tartine with Caramelized Onions and Sweet Currants

In the city, there is a tree-lined street on a hill dotted with cafes and wine bars, where cable cars run up and down the block. There is a restaurant on this street that I frequent. It's an intimate spot with dim lighting, cozy maroon seating and a menu that changes with the season. It's a place where I'm constantly mentally listing flavor combinations for future recipes.

One night I stopped in for dinner and out came a thick piece of sourdough bread that was toasted in fruity olive oil and topped with pieces of sautéed fish, cooked down with caramelized onions and slivers of almonds. I have yet to stop thinking about it. Here is an adaptation of that utterly delicious open-faced tartine.

SERVES 3–4

3 tbsp (45 ml) olive oil, divided

1 medium yellow onion, quartered and thinly sliced

Pinch of sea salt

Small handful of currants

Small handful of almonds, chopped, plus more for topping

¼ cup (60 ml) sherry vinegar

1 medium-sized piece of fresh tuna (I use ahi tuna), not canned

3–4 pieces of sourdough bread

In a medium-sized sauté pan over high heat, warm 2 tablespoons (30 ml) of olive oil for 1 minute. Add in the onions and sea salt. Lower the heat to medium-low and caramelize the onions for about 15 minutes. Add a few splashes of water if the pan dries out. Stir occasionally.

Add in the currants and almonds, and cook for another 3 minutes, stirring occasionally. Now add the sherry vinegar and cook for another 8 to 10 minutes, or until the sherry reduces down into the caramelized onions.

Rinse the tuna and pat it dry. Drizzle the remaining olive oil over the tuna on both sides and sprinkle with sea salt.

Once the onions have cooked, remove them from the sauté pan and set aside. Add the seasoned piece of tuna to that same sauté pan and cook on medium heat for about 5 minutes per side, or until the piece is fully cooked— seared on the outside yet slightly pink in the middle.

Once the fish is cooked, remove it from the sauté pan and set aside. Add the slices of sourdough to that same sauté pan. Warm both sides while collecting all the delicious juices from the cooked tuna and onions.

In a small mixing bowl, flake the tuna into small pieces and add the onion mixture. Mix everything until it's well combined.

Place the toast on a plate and top it with a heaping scoop of the tuna-onion mixture, a drizzle of olive oil and a few chopped almonds.

Tip: I use ahi tuna for this recipe but mackerel fish tastes just as great.

Stocking That Pantry

Having a well-stocked pantry is like having gas in the car, money in the wallet and a parking meter already filled with quarters. Pretty much all is possible with a pantry stocked with whole food goodness. Along with fresh fruits and vegetables, these are the staples that I turn to when cooking healthfully. If these ingredients are new to you, feel free to slowly incorporate them into your kitchen. I absolutely did not start off by throwing everything I already had into the trash. Rather when one item ran out, I replaced it with its healthier counterpart.

I'm also a big believer in getting the most out of your meals by utilizing spices. Adding spices is an effortless way of opening up a new world of cooking by transforming the humble vegetable with just a dash of cumin or a pinch of chili powder. To demystify this process, I've included a spice guide outlining the aromas and food pairings of familiar spices, keeping plant-based cooking exciting and doable.

Once you have a few staples in your pantry to play around with, cultivating a confident mindset toward this style of cooking is just as important. The three tips below helped me to reframe the way I viewed veggie-rich foods from one of "all salads are bland, so I'll pass" to that of creative encouragement.

Leave your comfort zone.

Try experimenting with different flavors, textures, aromas and seasonal produce. Explore the world of spices and see what flavors appeal to you.

Fill your dish with color.

Adding colorful ingredients to your plate ensures that you're eating a diverse range of plant-based goodness. Toss in anything from ruby red grapefruits to vibrant green avocados.

Take time to organize.

Set aside a few hours during the week dedicated to meal prep and stocking the pantry with foods that you know you'll enjoy later in the week.

Kitchen Go-Tos

Milk

Almond – A great nut milk that is neutral in flavor and goes well with nearly any food from savory to sweet.

Hemp Seed – My preferred homemade milk since there is no straining involved (recipe page 11)! You can find raw-shelled hemp seeds at most health food stores.

Coconut Milk – A delicious milk if you're looking for something more filling and sweet. I often use the cream portion of the milk to blend into desserts and make into whipped cream. I go for full-fat coconut milk.

Healthy Oils

Olive Oil – My most frequently used oil as it is mild in flavor and goes well with any vegetable dish. I use extra-virgin olive oil to top off salads.

Coconut Oil – When I can, I buy unrefined-extra virgin coconut oil as it retains more of its nutritional benefits in this form and also gives off a nice coconut aroma. This works great in stews and as a substitute for olive oil.

Ghee – Ghee is similar to clarified butter (butterfat with the milk solid removed) and is rich in flavor. It's great for sautéing vegetables as it has a high smoke point and delicious flavor.

Nuts + Seeds

I use more nuts than listed below but these are the ones I rely on most.

Almonds – Great for making homemade almond butter, milk or flour. Extremely versatile!

Cashew – This is my favorite nut butter spread. It is slightly sweet and often used in dessert recipes and in salad dressings, providing that creamy factor.

Pecans + Walnuts + Pistachios — These are my favorite nuts for dessert recipes. They taste great when roasted with a drizzle of maple syrup and cinnamon.

Tahini — Tahini is ground sesame seeds. It's often used to make hummus and creamy salad dressings. It can be found at most health food stores.

Pumpkin + Sesame Seeds — Both are great additions to salads, soups or stews as a crunchy topping.

Chia Seeds — A great egg substitute in recipes as it absorbs liquid and helps bind ingredients (recipe on page 188). They can be found at most health food stores.

Natural Sweeteners

Dates — I use Medjool dates as they are plumper and softer than other varieties. They are the dream snack. I take a few dates and stuff them with nut butter for a midday snack or before a workout. They also work great in dessert recipes as a sweetener and binding ingredient.

Honey + Pure Maple Syrup — These are great choices for liquid sweeteners.

Coconut Sugar — This is a great brown sugar substitute. It is rich in flavor with caramel undertones.

Whole-Grains

Oats — I buy rolled oats since it's easier to grind in a food processor/blender on the fly when oat flour is needed in a recipe. They're also an essential breakfast ingredient for porridge, bircher muesli, nut bars, etc.

Quinoa — This is a lovely grain to bulk up salads and is used as a rice substitute in curry and stew dishes.

Black + Brown + Wild Rice — All work great as white rice substitutes. Black and wild rice are a bit firmer in texture than brown.

Farro — Although farro contains gluten, I often use it in salads for a hearty addition.

Beans + Lentils

I use more beans than listed below but these are the ones I rely on most.

Butter Beans + Cannellini + Chickpeas — All work well in hummus recipes or when added to soups, stews and salads. All are neutral in flavor, which is great when adding spices to a meal as they absorb the flavor.

Black Beans — This is a great bean to have on hand and to toss into chilies, stews or soups. It has more of an earthy flavor than the beans above.

Red + Green Lentils — These are ideal for adding to soups and stews as they break down and become a bit tender in texture.

Black lentils — Perfect for salads as they retain their firm texture. They are milder in flavor than the lentils above.

Flours

Each one of these flours is available at health markets.

Spelt — Although spelt flour contains gluten, it is generally more easily digested than common wheat. I use this flour the most in baking recipes as a substitute for white flour.

Oat + Almond Flour — Both work well in baking and savory recipes since they're neutral in flavor.

Chickpea Flour — I use chickpea flour to make flatbread pizzas. And as a bonus, it is packed with protein and fiber, and is very inexpensive!

Arrowroot Powder — I use arrowroot in desserts as a natural replacement for cornstarch. This is also very inexpensive.

Herbs

Mint + Basil — These are great herbs that work well in sweet, savory and even smoothie recipes. Basil is great in pesto and pasta recipes, while mint can be used as a garnish to brighten up dishes.

Parsley + Cilantro — These are go-to herbs when finishing off savory meals, adding a touch of brightness to the dish. I often use the two interchangeably, although parsley is slightly bitter and cilantro is more pungent.

These are the spices that you'll see pop up most often and used together in recipes throughout the book.

Spices	Aroma	Spice Pairings	Food Pairings
Cumin	Deep, earthy aroma, with notes of pepper, very pungent	Works great when paired with other earthy spices: coriander, turmeric, pepper	An essential spice for stews, curries, chili and hearty vegetables
Coriander	A chameleon spice that combines sweet and earthy, with floral notes, and nutty when toasted	Pairs nicely with pepper, thyme, cilantro, cumin, ginger	An essential spice in curries and stews. Also pairs nicely in cookies and desserts as it lends a sweet aroma
Turmeric	Pungent spice, slightly bitter and musky with notes of citrus, ginger, mustard	Pair cumin, coriander and turmeric together for a homemade curry powder	An essential spice in masalas and curries, and pairs well with eggplants, beans, rice, quinoa
Chili Powder	A blend of spices that creates a robust aroma that is spicy and smoky	Works well with the above spices, garlic and oregano	Great in chili, soups and beans, or any time you want added heat
Garlic	Strong flavor that mellows when cooked, almost nutty	Pairs well with nearly anything savory: ginger, onions, chili, cumin, turmeric	Works well in nearly all savory dishes: curries, stir-fries, sauces, stews, soups
Ginger	Strong zingy flavor with brightness from lemony aroma	Works well with a variety of spices: garlic, coriander, lemongrass, lemon	Ideal in curries, stir-fries, dressings, and often paired with garlic
Cinnamon	Sweet, woody aroma	Works well with both sweet and savory spices: vanilla, citrus, cardamom, clove, nutmeg, coriander, turmeric	A great addition in any sweet dish (especially with chocolate) and in curries and stews, providing a warming note

For Extra Flavor

Each of these flavorings is available at health markets.

Sea Salt — I go for fine grain sea salt, usually Himalayan, as it's easy to measure and widely available.

Capers + Olives — Both provide a nice, salty flavor. I often use them together in salads, pasta sauces or in stews.

Lemon + Lime + Apple Cider Vinegar — I use these three interchangeably. I love finishing off a savory meal with zest of lemon or lime. A touch of zest also adds brightness to dessert recipes.

Curry Paste — Curry paste is made by ground spices and herbs often used in Thai cuisine. I buy curry paste from health markets as it's much more accessible than making curry paste from scratch.

Tomato Paste — A concentrated form of tomatoes, which means a little goes a long way. I add a tablespoon (15 g) to savory meals as it provides a very rich flavor.

Nutritional Yeast — A flaky, orange, non-dairy seasoning that mimics cheddar cheese! I absolutely love it in dishes where I want that cheesy element without the dairy. It is very inexpensive for a large bag.

Miso + Tamari — Both are fermented soybean products. I love adding both to boost flavors in Asian-inspired meals and soups. I also use tamari (gluten-free soy sauce) as a salt replacement in savory recipes. It gives a rich, umami flavor.

Vanilla Powder + Vanilla Extract — You'll see vanilla powder mentioned frequently throughout the book. Vanilla powder is more expensive, as its only ingredient is ground vanilla bean, making for a very pure aroma. Vanilla extract usually contains alcohol and, at times, gives off that aroma as well.

Fridge Staples

Nut Milk — I love having almond or hemp seed milk on hand. Making hemp milk from scratch is easy and also less expensive than almond milk (recipe on page 11).

Dijon Mustard — I use whole-grain Dijon in salad dressing all the time.

Tofu — I use organic tofu every so often and have found that extra-firm tofu works in recipes when you want to keep its firm texture. For creamy recipes, silken tofu is what you want to purchase. Both taste identical and are neutral in flavor.

Yogurt — I usually reach for Greek yogurt or coconut yogurt. Greek yogurt is more tart and is not vegan, while coconut yogurt is vegan (made from coconut milk) and sweeter. You can find both at health food stores.

Eggs + Fish — I'd recommend purchasing eggs that are organic, free of antibiotics and are non-GMO. When possible, try to source high-quality, wild-caught fish (salmon, shrimp, tuna, cod and halibut).

Freezer Staples

Fruit — I always keep a ton of pre-chopped (peeled) bananas and fruit in the freezer for a quick smoothie.

Veggies — I store bags of peas, green beans and sliced bell peppers in the freezer, and add them to soups and stews on the fly.

Pesto + Tomato Sauce — I almost never use the whole container, so I often store the extra in ice cube trays in the freezer for a later date. This way they're easy to pop out and use when I need a few for a recipe.

Egg Replacements

Both methods replace 1 egg in recipes.

Flax Egg: 1 tablespoon (7 g) of flaxseed meal + 2½ tablespoons (37 ml) of water. Stir and let sit for 5 minutes.

Chia Egg: 1 tablespoon (7 g) of ground chia seeds + 3 tablespoons (45 ml) of water. Stir and let sit for 5 minutes. You can also use unground chia seeds but the ground variety works better for thickening/binding purposes.

Equipment

I like to keep kitchen equipment simple. Most days I'll either use a food processor, high-speed blender or a microplane (used to zest citrus fruits or even cloves of garlic and ginger root). Those three are my go-to items. A hand mixer is convenient when making whipped coconut cream. If you plan to make almond milk, then you will need a nut bag strainer (available at health food stores or online), but if you make hemp milk, you don't need one (recipe on page 11)!

Thank You

Nearly three years ago, I started a food blog. I woke up every day, snapped a photo of my breakfast and posted it to Instagram. Never in my wildest dreams did I think any of this was possible. So thank you to my readers for your endless support! You inspire me every single day to keep on this wild path. It has been nothing short of amazing!

As much as this book is dedicated to my readers, it's also dedicated to my parents, my first supporters. You gave me the push and courage to pursue my dreams. To my mom, I always reflect back to that one winter night when you asked me, "What do you need to do to get to where you want to be?" You planted the seed that made all of this a reality. I am forever grateful. To my dad, my unofficial personal assistant, recipe tester and kitchen cleaner, *grazie* for all the last-minute trips to the grocery store for maple syrup and coconut oil. I know those moments drove you crazy but I could not have done this without you. To my beautiful sister Bridget, for always pushing me to be better and to see the light at the end of the tunnel. I won the family lottery with you three. Thank you to my entire family—my cousins, aunts, uncles and mama—for always being up to try my crazy recipes.

To Natasha, I know that none of this would have happened had it not been for your tireless encouragement. From supporting the blog in its infancy, to guiding me through this cookbook. I am so lucky to have you in my life! To my dearest Brittani, my life wouldn't be as full, exciting and full of love, had I not met you in Italy. Words cannot express how deeply lucky I am to have found you as my closest friend. This book wouldn't have happened had it not been for our late-night dinners and talks about life. To my amazing Stacy, your drive and pursuit for making the most out of what you have inspires me more than you will ever know. Thank you for your "woman-power," recipe ideas and last-minute edits! To Alyssa V and my cousin Alex, thank you for imparting your wisdom and wit during the creative moments of this book. To Jenny, for always leading me in the right direction—your advice is unparalleled. To Karen, for teaching me to always believe in myself and to be both a dreamer and a doer! And thank you for providing the photos of me throughout the book (karenbyrnes.com). Thank you to Mary Mar and Kristof from MMclay Ceramics for lending me your gorgeous ceramics for this cookbook. My food never looked so good!

And lastly to my amazing publisher and editor, Will and Marissa at Page Street. Thank you for taking a chance on me. If it weren't for that one email, which at the time I truly thought was spam, none of this would've been possible. You've made my dream a reality—expressing myself through food, photography and writing. Thank you from the bottom of my heart. And I am *so* happy that email wasn't spam!

Thank you, thank you, thank you!

xx Marie

About the Author

Marie Reginato is a food photographer, food writer, recipe developer and creator of the popular healthy food blog and Instagram account *8th and Lake.* Her recipes and photography have been featured by the likes of Jamba Juice, V8 Juice, Best Foods, Siggi's, Earthbound Farms, June Oven, thefeedfeed and MindBodyGreen. Marie has a degree in Agricultural Business from Cal Poly, San Luis Obispo. She is a native of San Francisco, California, and lives there today.

$\mathcal{I}ndex$